WORKSHOP

EN ROAD

THE PEOPLE

PEOPLE

THE PEOPLE

PEOPLE. USE IT

Poster Workshop 1968–1971

POSTERS

with information to
undermine all that
other information -
all that $ $ $ $.
resistance work . . .
join the poster
workshop - artists!
hands! money!
people & cheques to
the poster workshop

Poster Workshop 1968–1971

by Sam Lord,
with Peter Dukes, Jo Robinson *and* Sarah Wilson
with a foreword by Jess Baines

Four Corners Irregulars
N.º 3

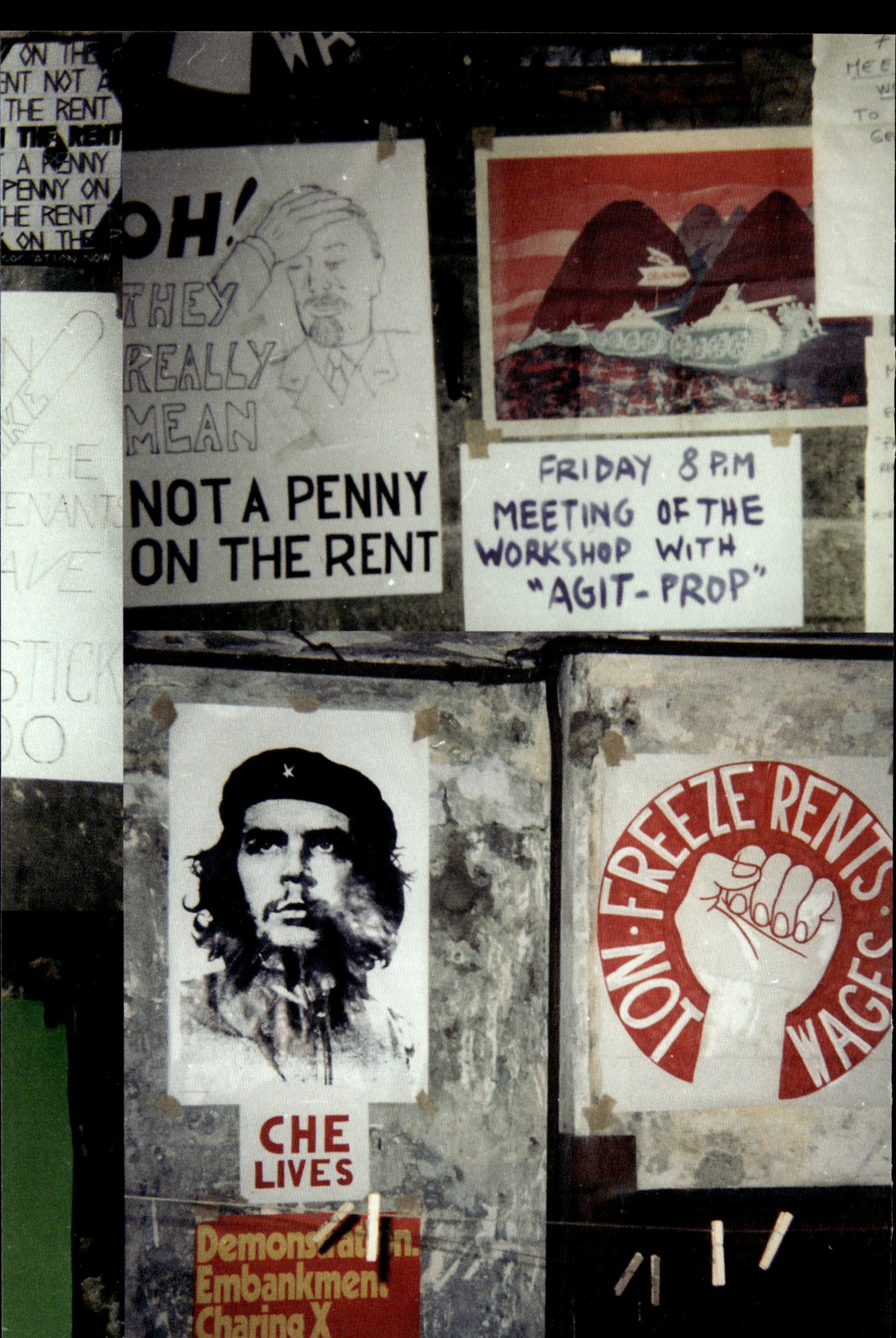
OH!
THEY
REALLY
MEAN
NOT A PENNY
ON THE RENT
FRIDAY 8 P.M
MEETING OF THE
WORKSHOP WITH
"AGIT-PROP"
CHE
LIVES
Demonstration.
Embankment.
Charing X
FREEZE RENTS.
NOT WAGES.
ON THE
RENT NOT A
THE RENT
I THE RENT
A PENNY
PENNY ON
THE RENT
ON THE
SOCIATION NOW
THE
ENANTS
AVE
STICK
DO
MEE
To
Ge

Contents

Posters on display at Poster Workshop premises.

POSTER WORKSHOP BENEFIT

c.a.s.t. - muggins awakening
& other plays
angry arts film society
- the columbia revolt
agit - prop street players

JAN 10 - 7.30

all saints hall
powis gardens
w.11

admission 5s

Foreword   *Jess Baines*

Impactful, mobile and populist in form, posters have long been used by political movements to agitate and publicise. However, in the late 1960s the activist poster was given a new lease of life through the use of screen-printing as a cheap, accessible and visually dynamic means by which to communicate. Often collaboratively produced, these posters, with their bold and densely inked slogans and graphics became the rapidly proliferating visual leitmotif of the protests that were unfolding around the world. Equipment in art schools was commandeered or even home-made and in a few instances self-sufficient workshops with a longer life were set up.

In Britain, it was Poster Workshop in London that first achieved this, making visible the new upsurge of left voices and causes of protest: from the war in Vietnam and apartheid in South Africa to racism and housing problems in London. Many of the posters that issued from the workshop are calls to action: Fight Factory Closures, March against the Shah, Demonstrate Against Racialism, Boycott California Grapes, Occupy Empty Property and of course, protest against the Vietnam War. Frequently they relate to specific campaigns and events; a demo, a picket, a meeting, a fundraiser, although there are general calls and statements too. Visually, some posters are the printed equivalent of an urgent and hastily written placard, whilst others reveal recognisable graphic skills, and perhaps more available time. Many are single colour, cheap and fast, with red and black predominating – the colours of leftist revolution. The iconography ranges from the tropes of clenched fist, crowd, prison bars and chains, to gruesome caricatures of targetted figures or artfully illustrated metaphors, as in *Cooking with Barbara* (p. 66) and *Spoonful of Sugar* (p. 68), both made in response to proposed anti-union legislation. What is striking is not only the diversity of political causes represented but also of visual styles. This is clearly reflective of the medley of politics, skills and aesthetic preferences amongst both Poster Workshop regulars and the many others that alighted on their resource. They were truly a people's workshop.

Poster Workshop benefit poster.

This activity was part of the ricochet of (mostly) youthful revolt taking place in many parts of the globe at this time, and 1968, the year of Poster Workshop's birth, was its highpoint. Born of a moment when radical ideas were in ferment and hopes for change were high, the history of Poster Workshop offers a compelling glimpse into a contradictory period of political, creative and social turbulence, when the forms of each – politics, art, society – and the boundaries between them were being challenged anew.

When in May-June 1968, thousands of French students occupied their universities, fought pitched battles with the police in Paris' Latin Quarter and triggered factory occupations and strikes by eventually ten million workers across the country, paralyzing the national government, a wave of hope that powerful political structures might be overcome infused young radicals around the world. Begun as a protest about the strictures and inadequacies of the university, a far wider radical political and social critique unfolded in the numerous assemblies and bulletins – as well as on the posters that were rapidly appearing on the streets. Students and artists had taken over the printmaking studios of the art schools, most famously in the Sorbonne's École des Beaux Arts, and set up ad-hoc radical poster-making factories, Ateliers Populaires (Peoples' Workshops), inspiring young radicals in other countries to do likewise.

Poster Workshop's existence converged with that of Britain's hippy counterculture. To some extent, both the growth of radical political ideas, groups and agitation and the more hedonistic, self-expressive proliferation of creative activities and lifestyles were all part of a general assault on prevailing values and institutions. Both also fuelled the instigation of 'alternatives' and counter-resources. Much of the counterculture was infused with a spirit of information sharing and do-it-yourself, necessary both for survival and for creating new ways of doing things outside of 'the system'. If understood as do it *ourselves*, this politically chimes with the notion of direct action, 'do-it-yourself' politics that was a feature of the community activist and housing struggles taking place in London, of which squatting is the most obvious example. Taken a little further it connects to the rallying cry of the strikes in May '68, autogestion: self management or self-organisation.

This was the working practice of Poster Workshop: working without bosses, and with an open-door policy, they invited people to come in and print their own posters. They provided 'how-to' instructions in the pages of the radical press (*Black Dwarf*, 1969) and offered to help people set up their own workshops. Other poster workshops did get started.

Advertisement for Poster Workshop.

POSTER WORKSHOP

61, CAMDEN ROAD, LONDON, N.W.1.

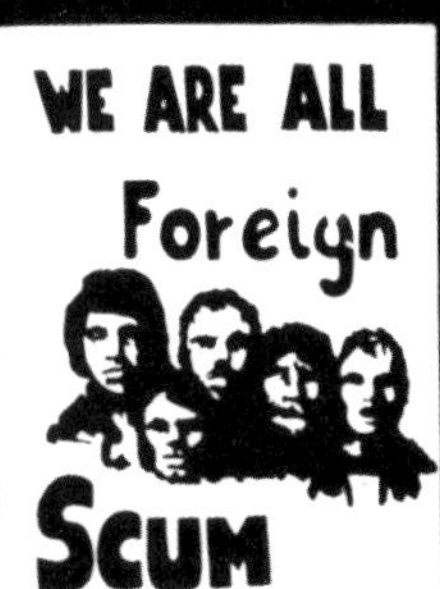

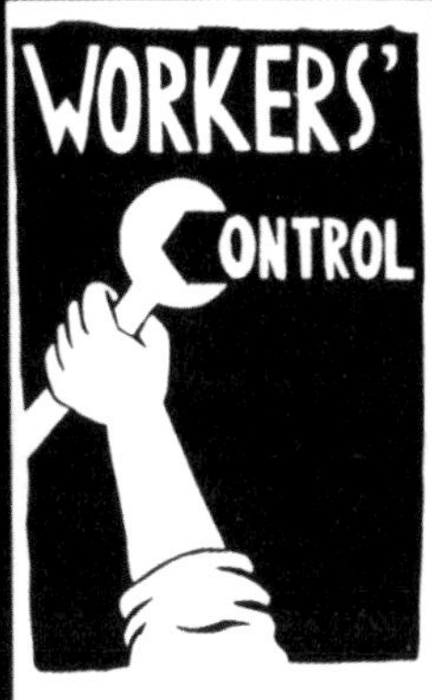

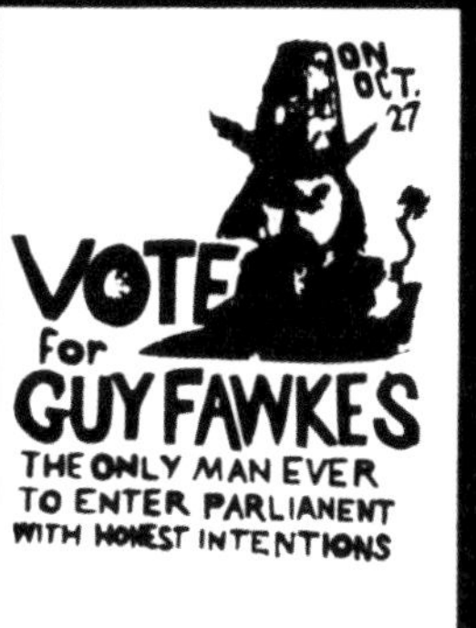

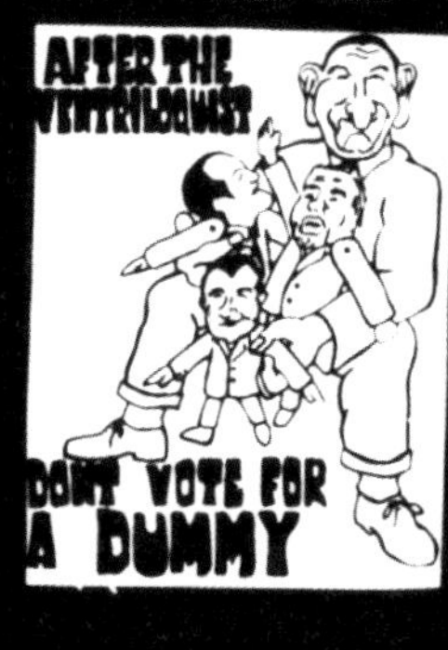

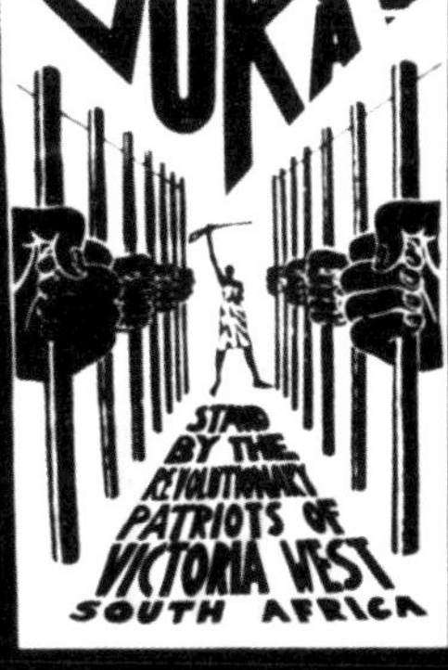

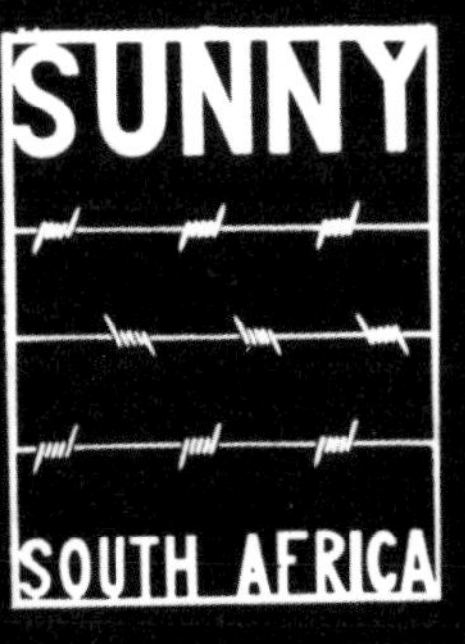

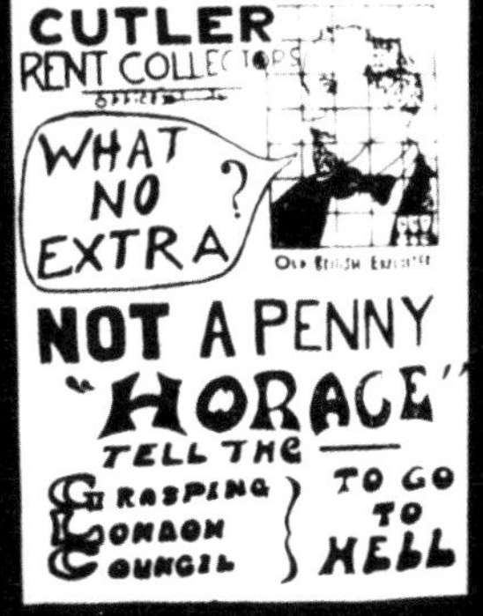

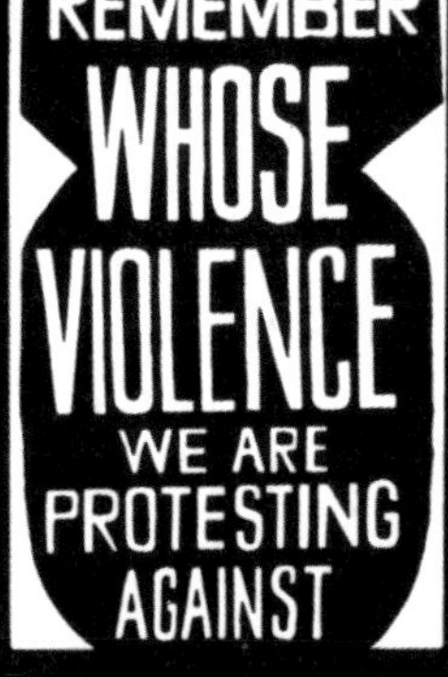

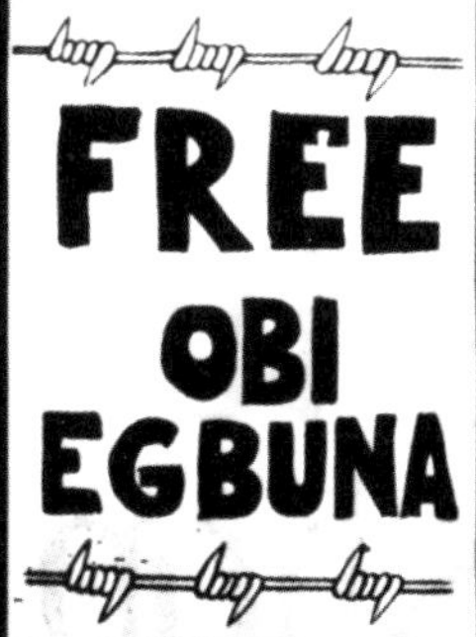

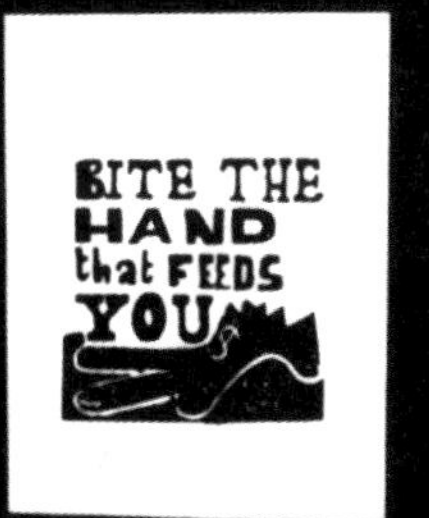

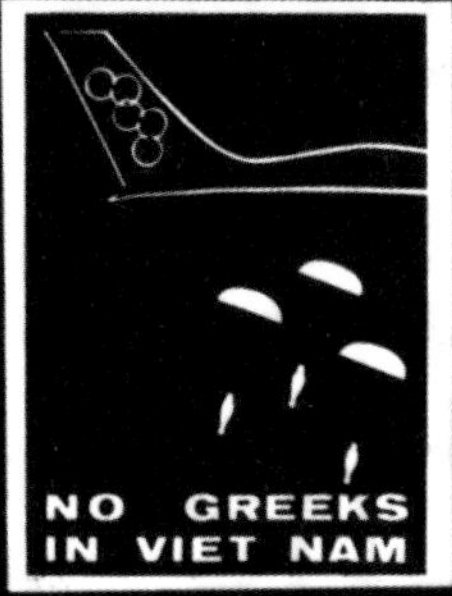

A notable instance, inspired by Poster Workshop's example and the Atelier Populaires, was set up in west London by Mike Braybrook in 1968. This was embedded in the local community activist scene and survived in various forms for many years. Also in 1968, another new type of 'peoples printshop' was established, a small offset-litho printers called Notting Hill Press. Here too, activists learned about the means of production, in this case for their leaflets, pamphlets and newsletters, as well as getting politically sympathetic – and cheap – printing. The real spread of sustained workshops however did not really happen until the 1970s. It is perhaps hard to envisage now, but being able to disseminate ideas and information that criticised powerful forces and prevailing values, especially on a low-to-zero budget, was not always easy. Print was the most accessible medium for people to use, but beyond the dilapidated duplicator, which was used mightily, amenable resources were typically scarce.

Radical poster-making fitted into a wider evolving field of politically motivated cultural production, which those same poster makers often also publicised. There were theatre and performance groups, such as CAST, Agit Prop Street Players and Welfare State all starting up in the late 1960s. These groups didn't just try and find new forms to raise political issues, but also took their performances to 'the people', on protests and pickets, in tenants and community halls and squats. There were film orientated groups too, such as the Angry Arts Film Society that organised screenings of political films, and Cinema Action who made films 'in the site of struggle' so that those involved in strikes for example could have their side of the story told, something almost entirely absent from mainstream media coverage. The question of form within different areas of cultural production as well as that of the audience's relationship was a point of debate. Many groups tried to break down the barrier between producers and audiences, either directly by developing participatory forms of production, or through setting up post performance/screening discussions. With regard to posters the question of aesthetics and message/audience could be a thorny one. In an issue of *Black Dwarf*, Roland Muldoon of CAST laid down the gauntlet when he suggested that the new radical posters appearing should use the most advanced technology and learn from techniques of capitalist advertising. The posters that issued from Poster Workshop clearly do not do that. Arguably many are more akin to what John Berger referred to in the late 1960s as necessary 'short-term works' of revolutionary propaganda which he argued 'must reveal in their structure and form their urgent but temporary function'. The posters were mostly made with the street in mind, for spaces and routes of agitational congregation (i.e. marches, occupations and pickets), for flyposting on targets, for organising protest. They were not generally made to be kept or sold as movement cultural commodities; those could be purchased from the back pages of the underground press. Slightly later groups, such as Poster Collective and See Red Women's Workshop would do this, indicating an evolution of the functions of the radical poster. The visibly basic means of Poster Workshop's output also signalled an accessible means of production, and as such acted as an implicit invitation to make your own propaganda – maybe even your own revolution.

Collaborative poster-making has been resurrected in an array of twenty-first century protest situations, proving itself once more to offer an accessible and salient form of activist communication and culture. As such it is especially exciting and relevant that this history of Poster Workshop has come to light, on paper. Fifty years on the posters in this book also provide a chance to reflect on how the struggles they depict have unfolded, on ways that we might work together, and what old and new languages visual, verbal and material are needed to articulate and mobilise, for now as then, *La Lutte Continue!*

Jess Baines is a Senior Lecturer at London College of Communication. She was part
of various radical printshops in London, including See Red Women's Workshop, Fly Press
and Calvert's Press.

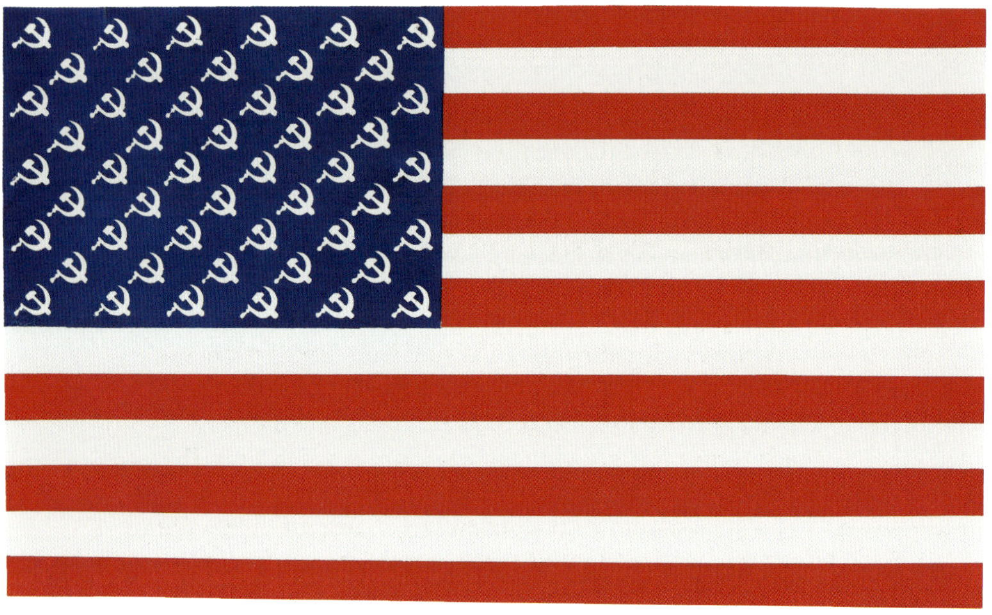

Poster Workshop

After leaving Art School in 1967, Sam Lord, already radicalised by the obscenity of the Vietnam War, shared a flat with others at 57 Moorhouse Road, Notting Hill Gate, then a rundown slum notorious for the misdeeds of exploitative landlords like Peter Rachman. It was here that Sam built a screen printing table in the kitchen where, along with Dick Pountain, he started printing various posters, including *Help we are Being Choked* (p. 30) and *Rent Infested* (p. 109), as well as one supporting the campaign to open up the locked garden in Powis Square for local use (p. 122). Prints were draped all over furniture, or laid out on the floor to dry and then fly posted in the neighbouring streets. In the spring of 1968, Sam met Peter Dukes, who was in the process of qualifying as a lawyer. They were introduced at a meeting of the Agitprop Information Service. Peter visited Moorhouse Road and helped to print posters there. Later, in June, they met Jean Loup Msika, a French Tunisian who had recently been expelled from France because of his involvement in the May events in Paris. As it turned out, his expulsion was only temporary – a campaign supported by Jean Paul Sartre and Simone de Beauvoir resulted in his return the following year, but not before the meeting with Jean Loup had provided the catalyst that led to the foundation of the Poster Workshop.

At the Atelier Populaire – the student-occupied print workshop at the École des Beaux Arts in Paris – Jean Loup had joined the group of artist activists producing posters supporting the student and worker demonstrations and occupations that were convulsing France in May 1968. They started using lithography, but soon changed to screen printing, which vastly increased the speed and economy of production. The resulting subversive posters were quickly printed, distributed and posted up all over the city to further the cause of the revolution – which, to all intents and purposes, was what Peter and Sam wanted to do in London.

Sickles and Stripes by Sam Lord, 1966.

Deciding to look for premises in order to increase the output, Peter found a cheaply available, but damp, cold and dirty basement at 61 Camden Road, London N1, beneath the Marylena hair salon. This was where the Poster Workshop was established with the transfer of the printing equipment from Moorhouse Road. Having brought over some samples of posters from the Atelier Populaire, Jean Loup used them to decorate the walls and the stairwell in order to provide inspiration and encouragement. The Poster Workshop was now open for business.

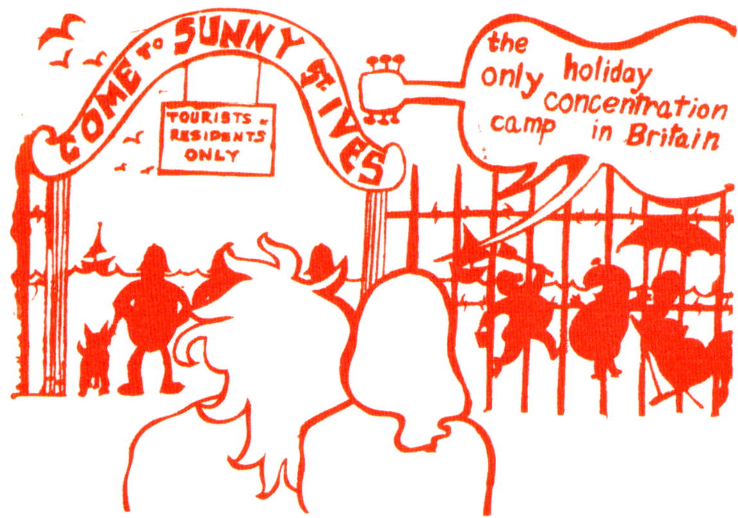

Buoyed up by a great deal of political enthusiasm, the fledgling Poster Workshop was able to flourish almost immediately as a vibrant source for radical and political posters in London and beyond. Its fame spread mainly by word of mouth. With very little basic training, anyone with a good enough cause could make posters, with or without assistance, and with or without a modest payment to cover costs.

Sam, Peter and Jean Loup were soon joined by others, including Ian Purdie who discovered the workshop and introduced a number of people, some of whom became indispensable members of the core group: Frederick Egbert Scrivener (Scriv for short), and in particular two art graduates, Jo Robinson and Sarah Wilson, without whose crucial continuous

Poster protesting against the exclusion of locals from the beach at St Ives.

commitment and contributions, the workshop would not have been able to function. Jo had become rapidly politicised overnight through meeting inspirational activists, while working as a scenic designer for the Unity Theatre in Mornington Crescent, and saw an opening for how art could be used politically. Sarah had returned from visits to Algeria, Paris and Cuba inspired by the Cuban quest for justice and equality.

No one received any payment for working at the Poster Workshop. Most participants were part time, and often had a paid job as well, or soon felt the need to find one, and so new volunteers were constantly needed. There were several other committed regulars, such as Alison Waghorn and Harry Beck. After leaving the merchant navy due to a long unresolved strike, Harry worked in a dry cleaning shop opposite the Poster Workshop. Intrigued by the sight of a succession of empty handed people entering the basement, but later emerging carrying piles of posters, he came over to investigate and quickly joined up. Unlike many others, Harry did not want to design any posters, but enjoyed printing them, and his seven years in the merchant navy had turned him into a cleaning dynamo. It gave him great satisfaction 'cleaning the deck', as he put it and trying to keep the workshop shipshape.

Special mention should be made of Scriv. He was a Cockney pensioner in his seventies who at that time saw himself in mortal combat with his declared arch enemy, Horace Cutler – 'Orrible Orace', the Tory Housing Committee chairman of the Greater London Council, a.k.a. the 'Grasping London Council', who in the eyes of Scriv and his comrades in many London tenants associations, was wickedly screwing residents out of their well-earned though meagre wages with steep and sudden rent rises. Fortunately, the Poster Workshop was able to supply them with an endless stream of radical propaganda; while a rejuvenated Scriv found a new career designing posters and working up his cartoons in his own special Scriv script with spotty capitals.

With his battered trilby perched on the back of his head, always dressed in a white shirt, waistcoat and tie – whatever the temperature or time of year – with a permanent rollup stuck to his bottom lip, and up to his ankles in highly inflammable rags, Scriv could be found at the Poster Workshop virtually every day fighting the good fight. He liked to believe that his efforts would lead to the collapse of the GLC. Ironically perhaps he was ultimately right, as it was indeed eventually abolished, for different reasons, by Margaret Thatcher. However, when it more or less forcibly rehoused Scriv in Brent, a long way from his beloved East End, he could no longer get to Camden in order to hold the fort, thereby inadvertently contributing to the closure of the Poster Workshop in 1971, for he had become all but indispensable.

Scriv had a long, colourful history, leaving him with many interesting reminiscences: In 1926 during the General Strike, he managed to change a strategically placed railway signal at Kings Cross to indicate Stop! He went on to help to tip coal from the stationary wagons off the bridge onto the street below for people to collect to heat their homes.

Functioning of the Poster Workshop

Peter was the Poster Workshop's organisational genius. Having a particular talent for planning and management, he ensured there was always a good supply of materials. Oil based printing inks, brushes, stencil materials, craft knives, adhesives, masking tape and cleaning fluids were bought from Screen Process Supplies in Parsons Green just off Fulham Road, while most reams of paper were collected by him in his Mini from relatively cheap suppliers in the East End of London.

Occasionally, large quantities of unwanted posters were donated free of charge including versions of the famous *Your Country Needs You* poster featuring Lord Kitchener. Originally printed during the First World War, they were more prosaically reprinted as publicity for the fashion boutique I Was Lord Kitchener's Valet in Carnaby Street. The use of these posters demonstrated an early, if unconscious, support for recycling when the Poster Workshop printed new images on Lord Kitchener's still white backside.

It was Poster Workshop policy to enable as many people as possible to learn the necessary skills to make posters and any radical person or group was free to design and print their own posters. However, if they didn't feel confident enough, there were always people available to help, or even to do the work on their behalf. Slogans and copy were usually provided by those requiring posters, but sometimes an excessively worded poster could be improved with a succinct slogan and a strong visual image.

When representatives of a group requested a poster of questionable political validity, an informal ad hoc meeting was held by whoever happened to be around at the time in order to come to a democratic decision. In fact, many decisions were made this way, though from time to time larger meetings were also held. But on the whole, the Poster Workshop happily ran itself.

Poster in support of striking workers made at Poster Workshop.

UNITY IS STRENGTH

There were no fixed or imposed charges for posters. Groups paid what they felt they could afford towards the cost. Funds were augmented occasionally by donations and benefit shows given, for example, by CAST (Cartoon Archetypal Slogan Theatre), and by the Agitprop Street Players (soon to be renamed Red Ladder Theatre). Peter, as well as manning the Poster Workshop, also managed to be an active founder member of the Street Players. In practice, voluntary payment meant that some groups, such as tenants associations, factory workers and trade unions, paid scrupulously, though rarely lavishly, while other less organised groups, like student associations, were not so reliable in their contributions. One of our number also helped pay the rent.

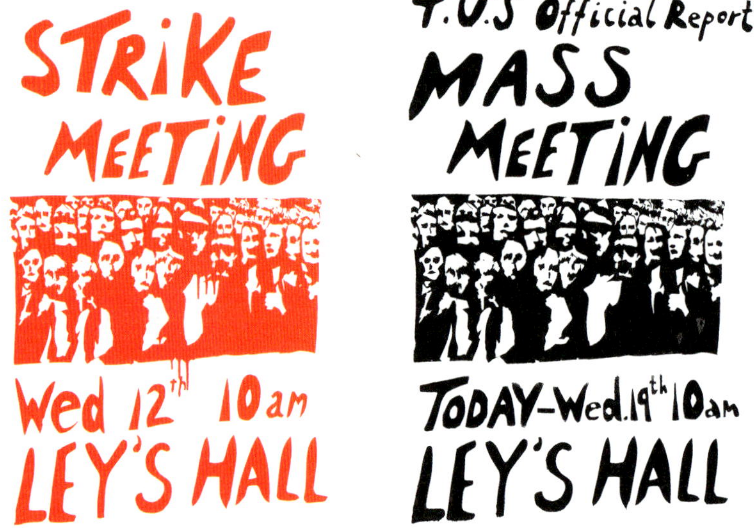

The Poster Workshop could, if necessary, respond very rapidly to a request for posters. The most extreme case was in response to an industrial dispute at Ford's, Dagenham. The vote to strike had been taken at 10 p.m., following which shop stewards rang through for posters to be made available for the start of the morning shift at 6 a.m. The Poster Workshop worked all night, designing, printing and finally drying hundreds of posters with hair dryers fortuitously borrowed from the Marylena hair salon for another urgent run. The posters were then driven out to Dagenham in the small hours of the morning just in time for the arriving workforce to be informed of strike action before the start of the morning shift.

Above: Posters for Dagenham strike. Opposite: Poster Workshop premises.

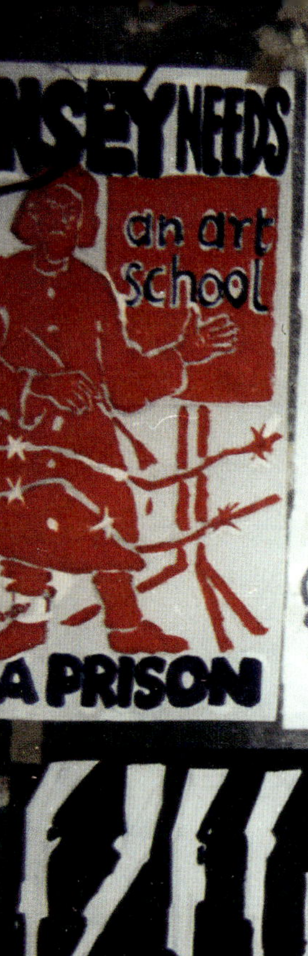

...SEY NEEDS
an art
school
A PRISON

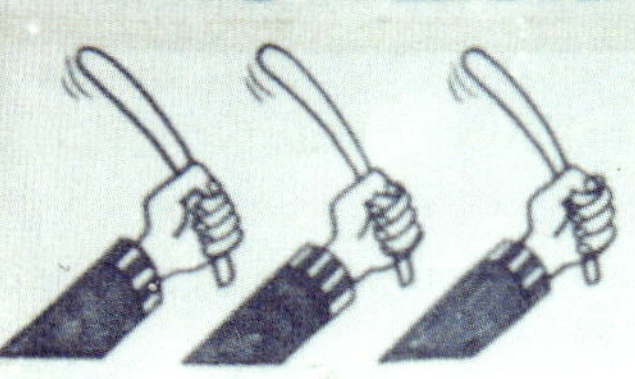

"A CAUSE FOR
CONCERN"
FREE OBI EGBUNA
(JAILED FOR ATTEMPTING TO
ORGANIZE SELF DEFENSE
OF BLACK PEOPLE FROM
POLICE VICTIMIZATION)

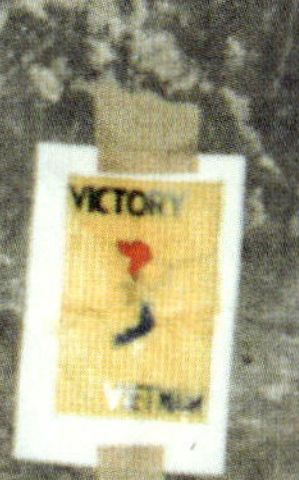

VICTORY
VIETNAM

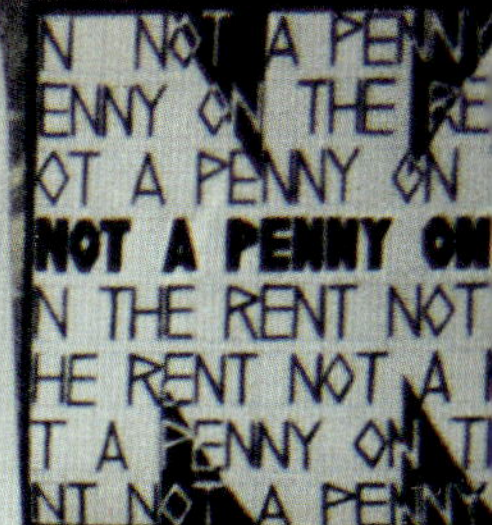

N NOT A PENNY
ENNY ON THE RE
OT A PENNY ON
NOT A PENNY ON
N THE RENT NOT
HE RENT NOT A
T A PENNY ON T
NT NOT A PENNY

DEAR N.F.
WE'RE FIGHTING THEM
TOO

RENT MA
TREAD
SOFTLY
BIG
TO

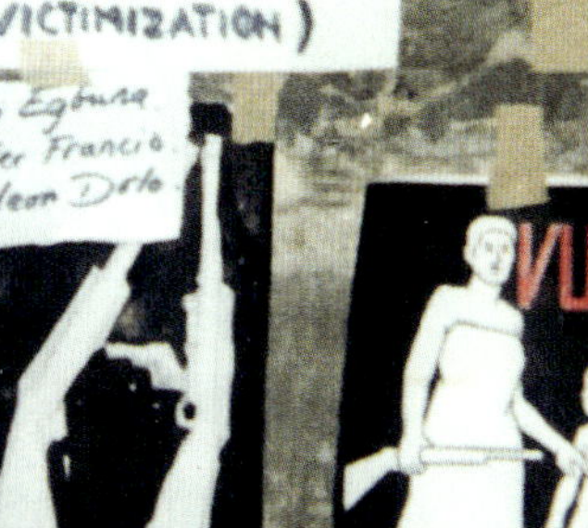

VUKA

Obi Egbuna
Peter Francis
Gideon Dolo

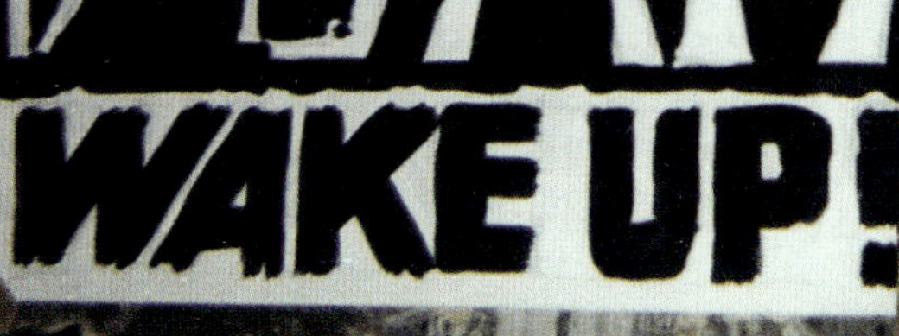

WAKE UP!

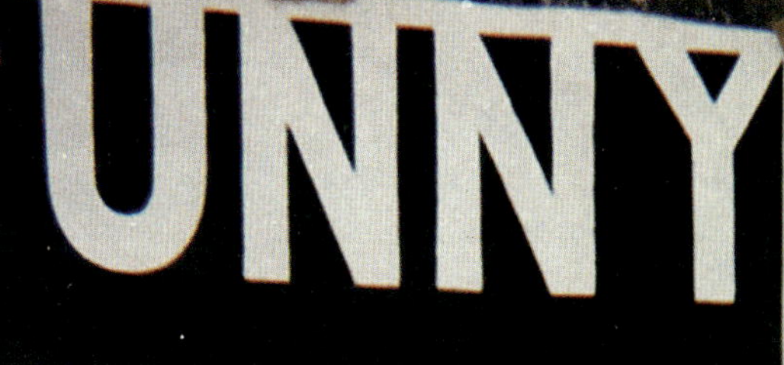

SUNNY

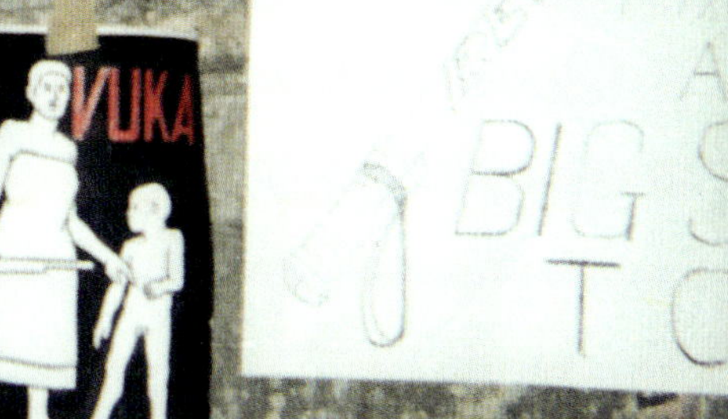

A MEETING OF
AMERICAN
RADICALS
THE

All kinds of people came to the Poster Workshop: GLC tenants associations protesting against steep rent rises, striking workers, anti-apartheid groups, CND, International Socialist groups, Young Communists (and some older ones as well), anti-Vietnam war groups, South African anti-Apartheid and liberation organisations such as the ANC (African National Congress) and the PAC (Pan African Congress), other liberation movements, supporters of civil rights, Black Power groups, the Californian Farm-Workers Union, The London Fire Brigade Union, Irish groups, radical film and theatre companies, anarchists, Situationists, radical journals like *Black Dwarf*, and many different student organisations.

Travelling Poster Workshop

Screen printing does not require heavy or expensive equipment, so it is easy to transport and to function almost anywhere. Now and again, additional Poster Workshops were set up when requested in other places, not only to print posters, but also to show people how to make them. The first Poster Workshop to travel was installed by Sam Lord, Pete Binns and Dick Pountain in the refectory at the London School of Economics during its occupation by students prior to the much hyped anti-Vietnam war march on 27 October 1968. They were soon joined by Peter Dukes, Jo Robinson and Sarah Wilson.

As ever, anyone interested could design a poster. A large number were printed, mounted on boards, attached to batons and later carried as placards on the march. The atmosphere at the LSE was one of vibrant enthusiasm, unclouded by academic demands. In the event, only three of the posters designed there directly targeted the Vietnam War – *UK 51st State of the US* (p. 41), *We Must Push Back, Pull Out and Break the Fangs of Capitalism* (p. 31) and *Remember Whose Violence we are Protesting Against* (p. 40). A few days prior to the planned demonstration during a debate in the House of Commons concerning his proposal to amend the 1936 Public Order Act, paranoid right wing Conservative MP for Ilford North, Tom Iremonger, had said, 'The British People are fed up with being trampled underfoot by foreign scum'. So the LSE workshop quickly responded with more posters – *We are all Foreign Scum* (p. 85), and *Vote Guy Fawkes – The Only Man to Enter Parliament with Honest Intentions* (p. 44), as well as *Puritanism will Castrate our Revolution* (p. 26).

In the snowy February of 1969, Peter, Sam, Jo and Sheila Rowbotham went on missions to Essex University. Their intention was to teach the more militant students how to screen print.

Promotional poster at Poster Workshop premises.

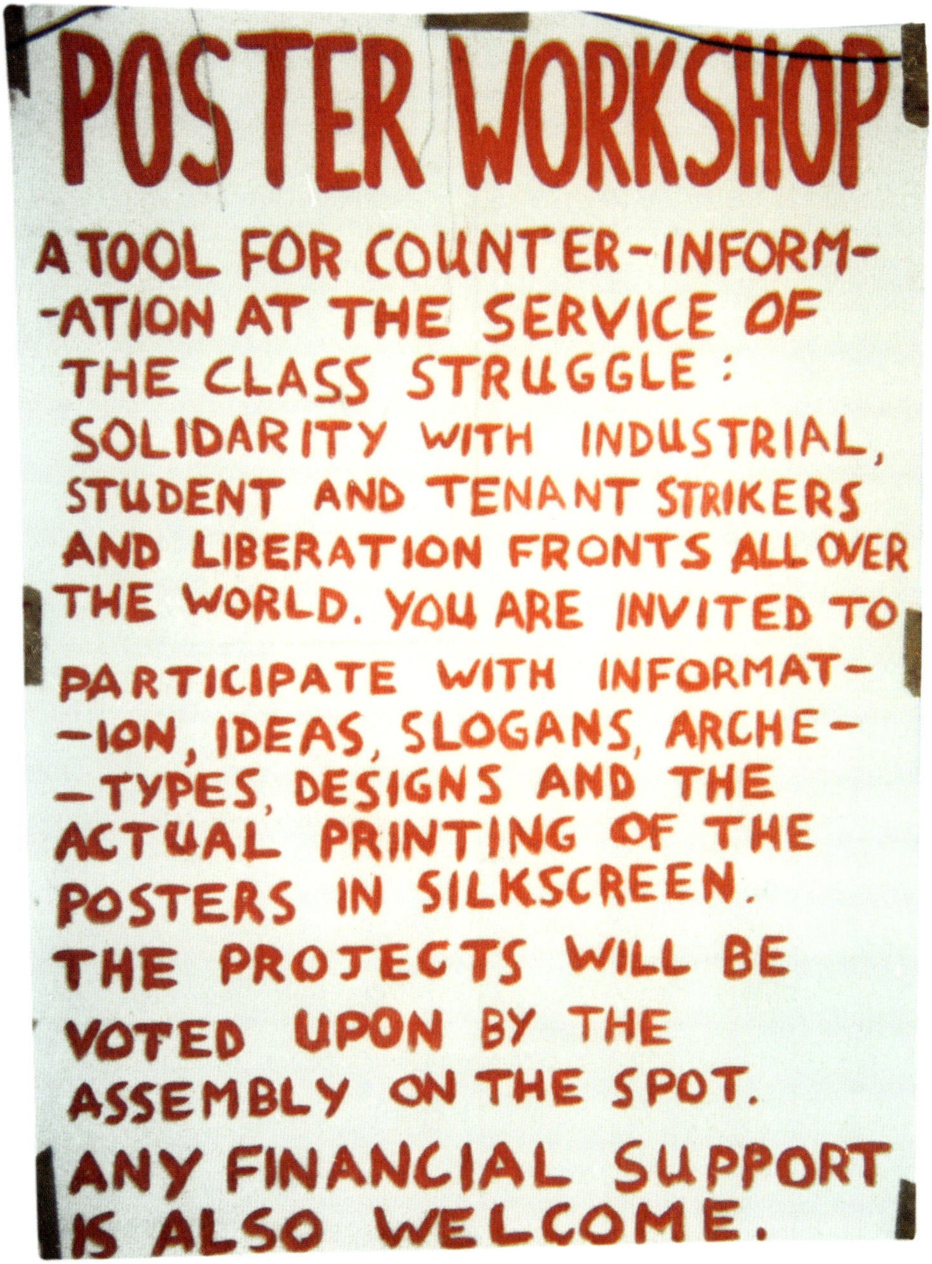

POSTER WORKSHOP
A TOOL FOR COUNTER-INFORM-
-ATION AT THE SERVICE OF
THE CLASS STRUGGLE:
SOLIDARITY WITH INDUSTRIAL,
STUDENT AND TENANT STRIKERS
AND LIBERATION FRONTS ALL OVER
THE WORLD. YOU ARE INVITED TO
PARTICIPATE WITH INFORMAT-
-ION, IDEAS, SLOGANS, ARCHE-
-TYPES, DESIGNS AND THE
ACTUAL PRINTING OF THE
POSTERS IN SILKSCREEN.
THE PROJECTS WILL BE
VOTED UPON BY THE
ASSEMBLY ON THE SPOT.
ANY FINANCIAL SUPPORT
IS ALSO WELCOME.

Early that summer, Jo and Sarah traveled with Ian Purdie to an island on Loch Corrib in Galway in the west of the Republic of Ireland, where the playwrights John Arden and Margaretta d'Arcy lived with their four boys. They were involved with the Land League, which was set up in the 19th century to fight for tenants' rights against exploiting landlords, but now wanted posters for a campaign against the sale of good farming land to large conglomerates to create golf courses. Posters were designed and printed on a table in the open air, and then hung up to dry on lines strung between trees. The Land League were very secretive about their identity; two men rowed out to the island and when the posters had dried they took them and all traces of them – rough drawings, stencils etc. – and rowed away into the night. Unfortunately we have no record of these posters.

Later that summer, People's Democracy asked the Poster Workshop to go to Free Belfast and Free Derry in the north of Ireland. People's Democracy was a political organisation which supported the campaign for civil rights for the Catholic minority, and believed that this could only be totally achieved through a United Socialist Republic of Ireland. Nationalist enclaves, protected by barricades, had been set up following attacks on Catholic areas by Loyalists and Protestant paramilitary B-Special police, and were run by citizens groups and the Republican movement, working with People's Democracy. So Sarah went over in a car loaded with equipment. Two small rooms on the ground floor of a terraced house in the Lower Falls were provided, one for making posters, the other for hanging them up to dry. Upstairs, Radio Free Belfast transmitted news and record requests. Next door was a very busy pub; further along the street, in a small community centre a board was put up inviting people to write down ideas for slogans. They were checked every day, and the best selected for new posters.

The messages that People's Democracy wanted to focus on were that the establishment was the real enemy, not the Protestant Loyalists, and that the barricades should be maintained, which the media and the government were urging people to remove on the grounds that they were no longer required now that the British Army had been mobilised to protect them!

The demand for posters was enormous. Everything produced was posted up around the city. There was urgency and energy, with requests for new posters constantly coming in, and queues forming to put up fresh batches.

After a few weeks in Belfast, a number of locals had become proficient enough to keep production going, so Sarah moved on to Derry to start up another workshop there. In both cities she was housed and fed by members of People's Democracy.

While Sarah was working in Derry, the British Army arrested three people in Belfast for fly-posting, handing them over to the Royal Ulster Constabulary. They were taken to court and given prison sentences, one for three months. This was shocking, for in England no one got more than a fine for fly-posting. In fact, these were the first arrests that the army made in the north of Ireland. Subsequently, a number of letters were written to the newspapers pointing out that far more provocative posters had been made and put up by the loyalist community, but had been ignored. A poster, showing hands behind bars, was rapidly printed with the slogan *Army Protection* (p. 119). This was posted up in many places, including the spot where the arrests had been made.

Demise and Future

The Poster Workshop continued to function until 1971, but eventually folded because it had come to rely, perhaps excessively, on Scriv to permanently man the basement, and he had now been rehoused in Brent. Other volunteers had taken full time employment, or had become involved in other causes, such as Claimants Unions and Women's Liberation groups. A number of organisations, such as *Black Dwarf* magazine, edited by Tariq Ali, and the International Socialists, had bought relatively inexpensive off-set litho presses, allowing them to print posters for themselves and for others at relatively affordable commercial rates. Even so, nothing could compare with the low to zero rates offered by the Poster Workshop.

The Poster Workshop existed at an exceptional time, thriving on the energy generated by the belief that huge changes were possible – indeed were already taking place around the world through movements for equality, civil rights, freedom, democracy and revolution. To many it seemed as if capitalism deserved to be smashed, could be smashed and would be smashed. Alas a premature dream! Today the capitalist system is more entrenched than ever due to an increasingly strident belief in the sacred power of market forces and industrial production. It is a system that is still the regular cause of crises all over the world – oil inspired wars, financial meltdown threatening economic collapse, and environmental disaster. A system still capable of doing little more than merely stagger along; but as always 'it's the rich what gets the pleasure and the poor wot gets the blame'.

Making the Revolution

Many of the posters in this section were influenced by Situationist International, a very small group of social revolutionaries composed of avant-garde artists, intellectuals and political theorists. Founded in 1957 and dissolved in 1972, the Situationists were anti-authoritarian Marxists inspired by early 20th century art movements, especially Dada and Surrealism. As time passed, the movement drifted from art towards political action. They believed that workers in an advanced capitalist society still worked merely to survive in a world where technological efficiency had hugely increased productivity. The purpose of capitalism is not freedom or happiness, but simply more and more production. Production as an end in itself. Work becomes more and more efficient, yet more and more meaningless, leading to alienation. Capitalism encourages mass consumption and, in order to disguise the alienation and lack of purpose in life, invents the spectacle, where the media increasingly takes over and replaces authentic experience. Life is reduced to an immense accumulation of spectacles, the triumph of appearance over substance. 'All that was once directly lived has become mere representation'. (In 1968 Britain had just three TV companies and only one, BBC Two, had begun broadcasting in colour. Phones were firmly attached to the wall with flex and there were no personal computers). Situationist thinking disproportionately influenced the May events in France, but also the Angry Brigade in London, the Amsterdam Provos and the Weathermen in the US. The Angry Brigade made a series of bomb attacks in the early 1970s (small bombs to minimize collateral damage), targeting far right regimes, the army, the police, the houses of Cabinet Ministers, the Miss World Competition and property speculators. 25 attacks were made, one person was slightly injured. Those found guilty got 10 years.

The two *Street Fighting* posters (pages 25 and 26) reflect the Rolling Stones hit 'Street Fighting Man'. *Help we are Being Choked* (p. 30) was printed at Moorhouse Road. *Puritanism will Castrate our Revolution* (p. 26) was printed at the LSE as a warning against centralised control.

'... THE
TIME IS
RIGHT FOR
FIGHTING
IN THE
STREETS'

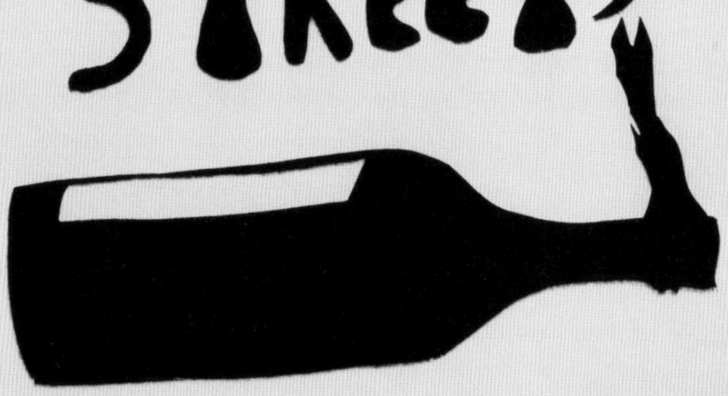

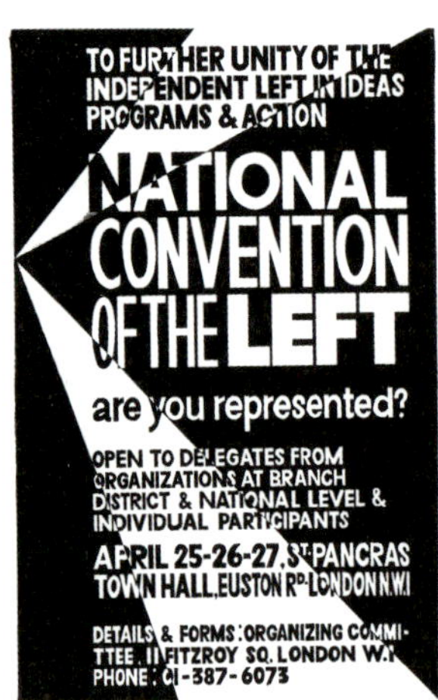

TO FURTHER UNITY OF THE INDEPENDENT LEFT IN IDEAS PROGRAMS & ACTION
NATIONAL CONVENTION OF THE LEFT
are you represented?
OPEN TO DELEGATES FROM ORGANIZATIONS AT BRANCH DISTRICT & NATIONAL LEVEL & INDIVIDUAL PARTICIPANTS
APRIL 25-26-27, St. PANCRAS TOWN HALL, EUSTON Rd. LONDON N.W.1
DETAILS & FORMS: ORGANIZING COMMITTEE, 11 FITZROY SQ. LONDON W.1
PHONE: 01-387-6073

'SUMMERS HERE & THE TIME IS RIGHT FOR FIGHTING IN THE SREETS...'
WHAT ARE YOU DOING HERE?.... DO YOU THINK YOU CAN ESCAPE FROM THE SYSTEM...?
FUCK THE SYSTEM, IT FUCKS YOU

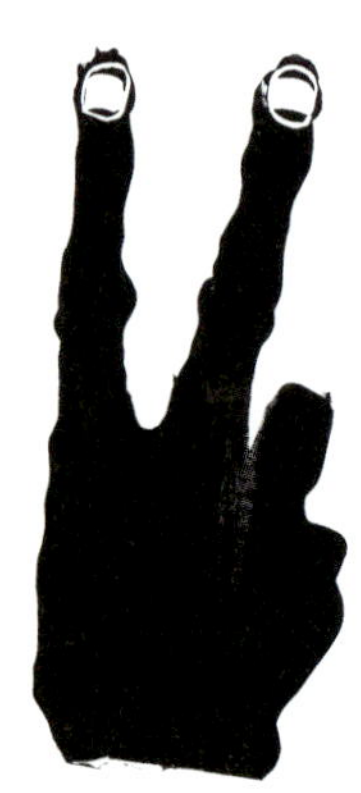

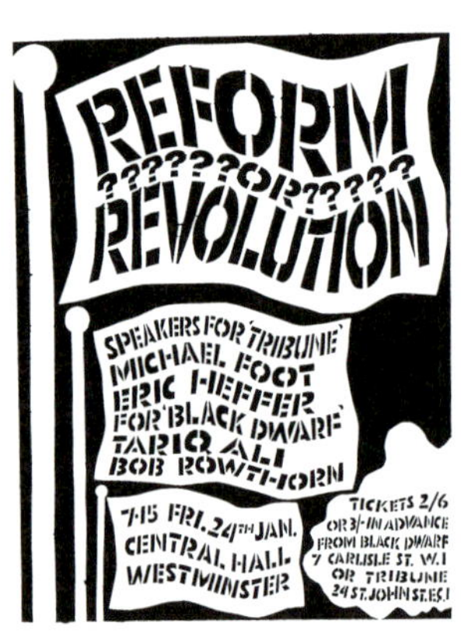

REFORM ??????OR?????? REVOLUTION
SPEAKERS FOR 'TRIBUNE' MICHAEL FOOT ERIC HEFFER
FOR 'BLACK DWARF' TARIQ ALI BOB ROWTHORN
7.15 FRI. 24TH JAN. CENTRAL HALL WESTMINSTER
TICKETS 2/6 OR 3/- IN ADVANCE FROM BLACK DWARF 7 CARLISLE ST. W.1 OR TRIBUNE 24 ST. JOHN ST. E.C.1

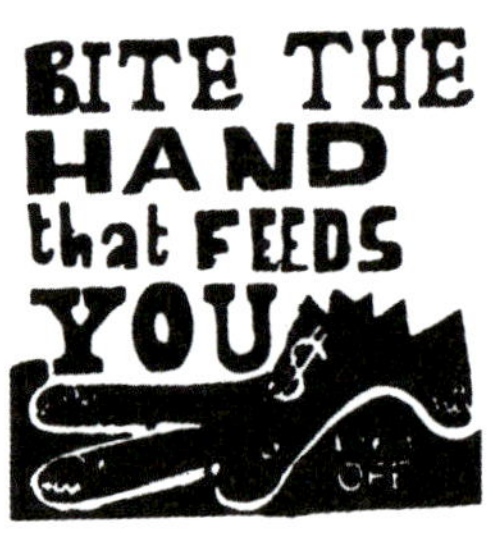

BITE THE HAND that FEEDS YOU

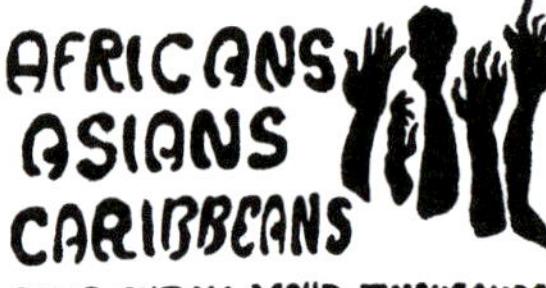

AFRICANS ASIANS CARIBBEANS
COME OUT IN YOUR THOUSANDS
DEMONSTRATE AGAINST RACIALISM DURING THE COMMONWEALTH PREMIERS CONFERENCE
SUN JAN 12 1969 ASSEMBLE 2 PM
HYDE PARK   SPEAKERS CORNER
MARCH WITH THE BLACK PEOPLE'S ALLIANCE

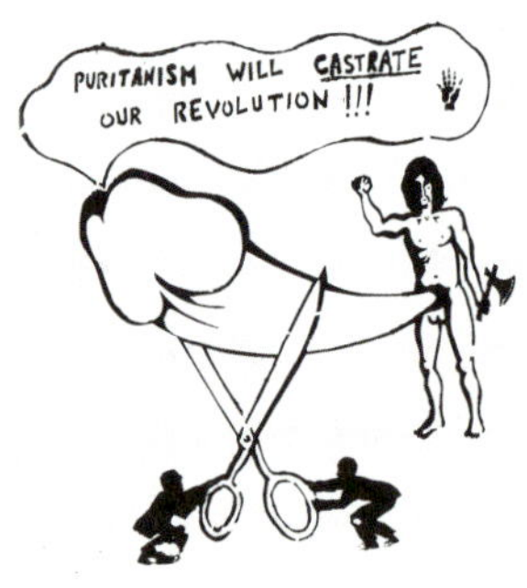

PURITANISM WILL CASTRATE OUR REVOLUTION !!!

PUBLIC MEETING
MONDAY JUNE 28   8 PM
CAN LABOUR BRING SOCIALISM
STAN NEWENS . PAUL FOOT
MOZART HOUSE   66 ALBION RD N.16

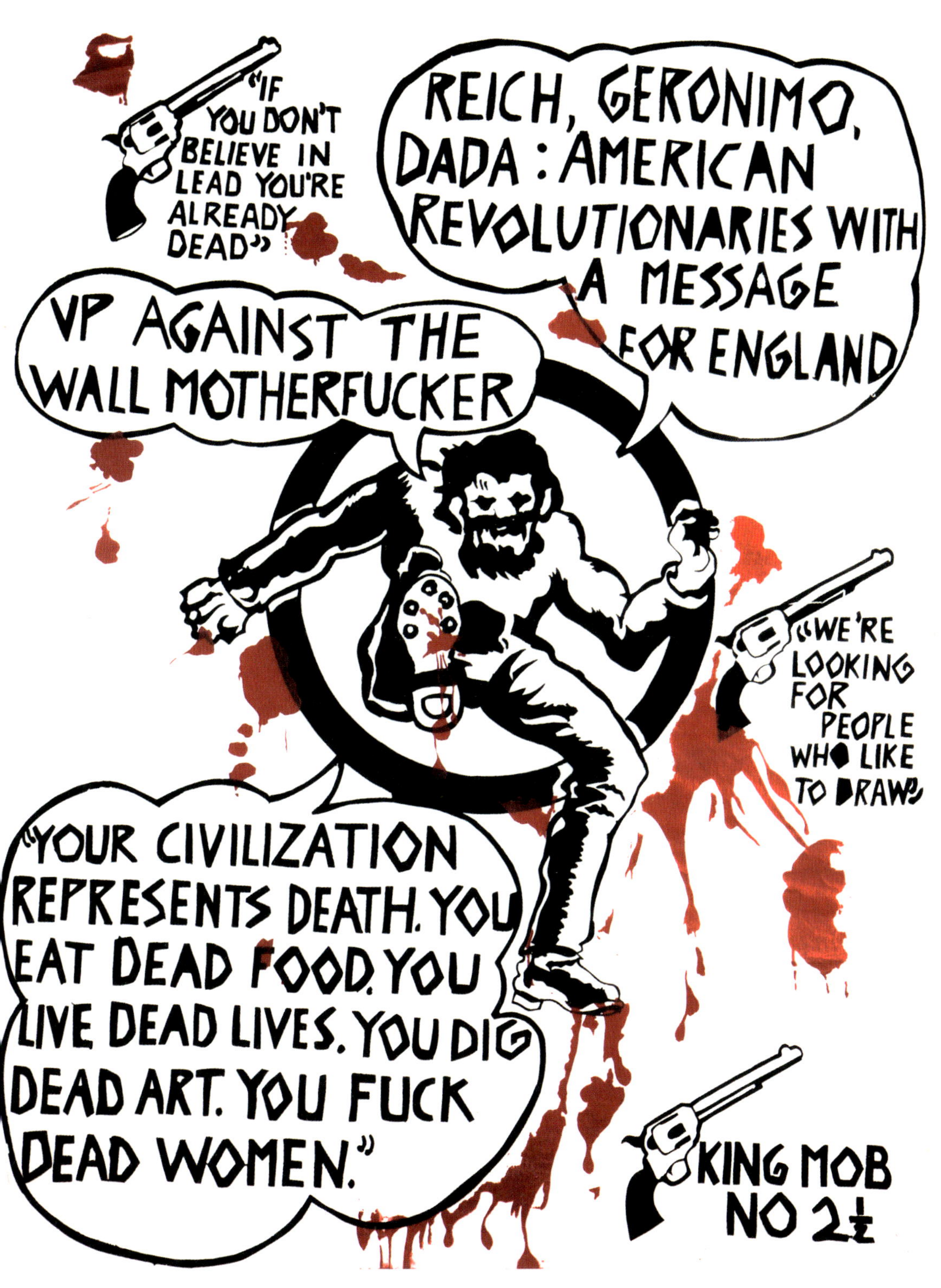

"IF YOU DON'T BELIEVE IN LEAD YOU'RE ALREADY DEAD"
REICH, GERONIMO, DADA: AMERICAN REVOLUTIONARIES WITH A MESSAGE FOR ENGLAND
UP AGAINST THE WALL MOTHERFUCKER
"WE'RE LOOKING FOR PEOPLE WHO LIKE TO DRAW"
"YOUR CIVILIZATION REPRESENTS DEATH. YOU EAT DEAD FOOD. YOU LIVE DEAD LIVES. YOU DIG DEAD ART. YOU FUCK DEAD WOMEN."
KING MOB NO 2½

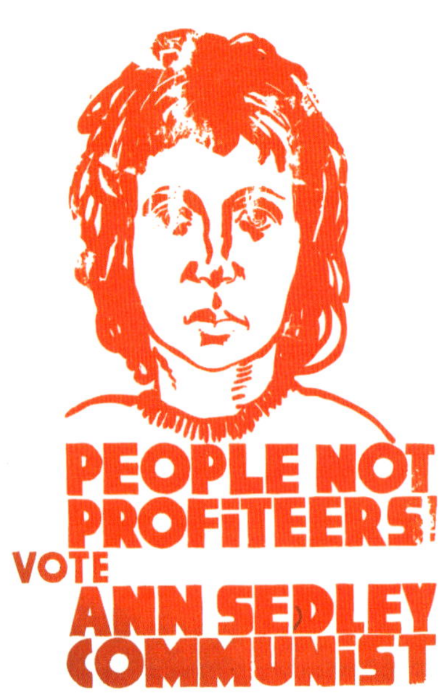

PEOPLE NOT
PROFITEERS!
VOTE
ANN SEDLEY
COMMUNIST

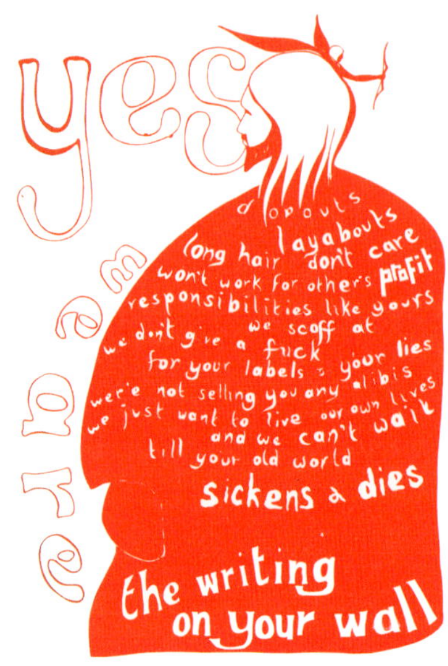

yes
we are
dropouts
long hair layabouts
won't work for others profit
responsibilities like yours
we don't give a fuck
we scoff at
for your labels & your lies
we're not selling you any alibis
we just want to live our own lives
and we can't wait
till your old world
sickens & dies
the writing
on your wall

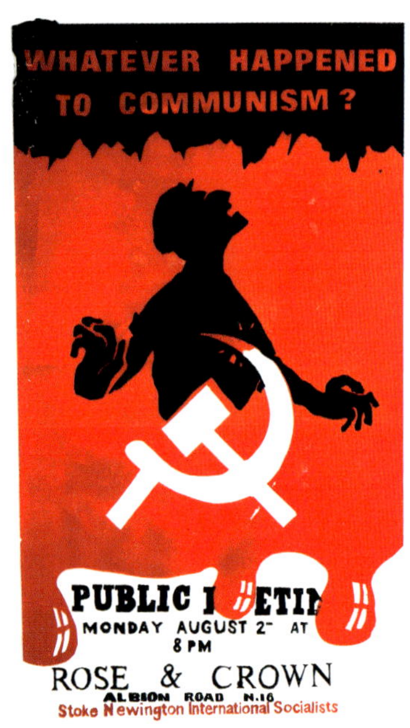

WHATEVER HAPPENED
TO COMMUNISM?
PUBLIC MEETING
MONDAY AUGUST 2ⁿᵈ AT
8 PM
ROSE & CROWN
ALBION ROAD N.16
Stoke Newington International Socialists

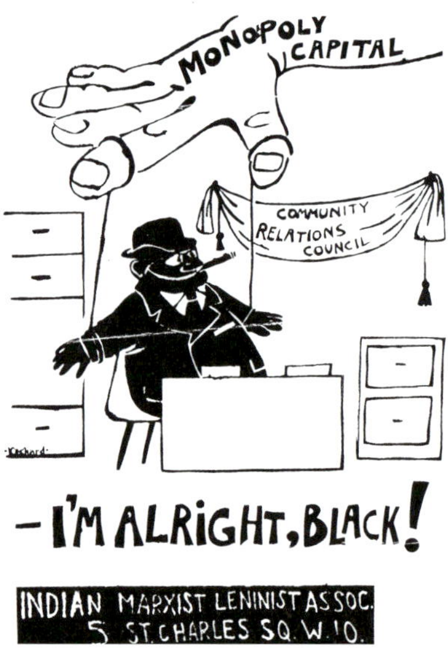

MONOPOLY CAPITAL
COMMUNITY
RELATIONS
COUNCIL
-I'M ALRIGHT, BLACK!
INDIAN MARXIST LENINIST ASSOC.
5 ST CHARLES SQ. W.10.

REVOLUTION '68

HELP! WE ARE. BEING choked

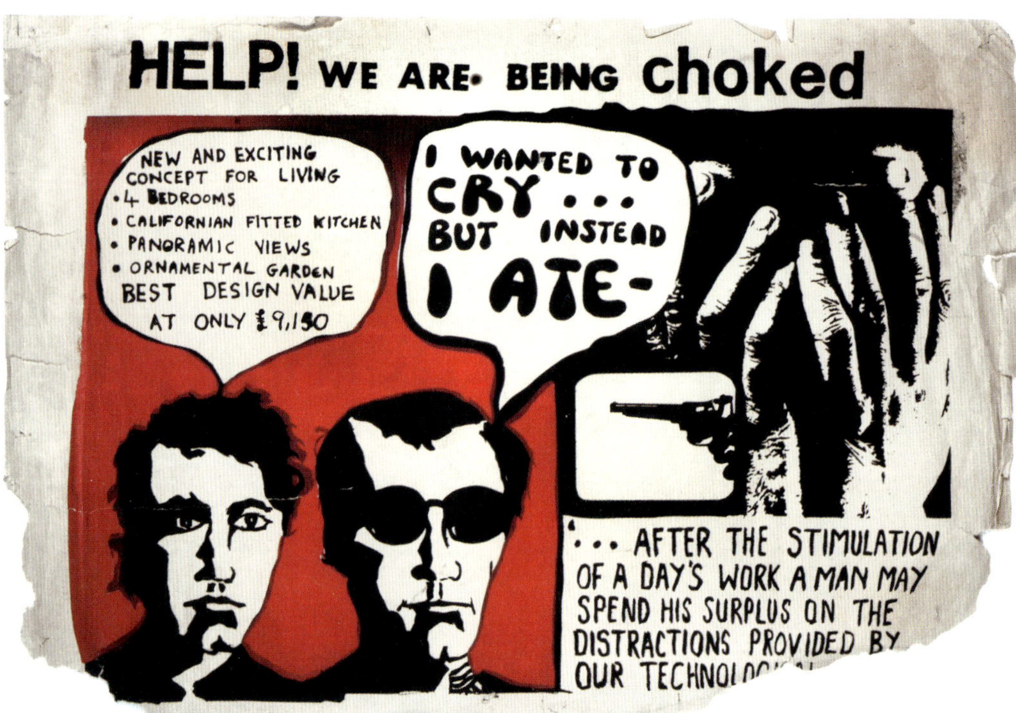

WE MUST

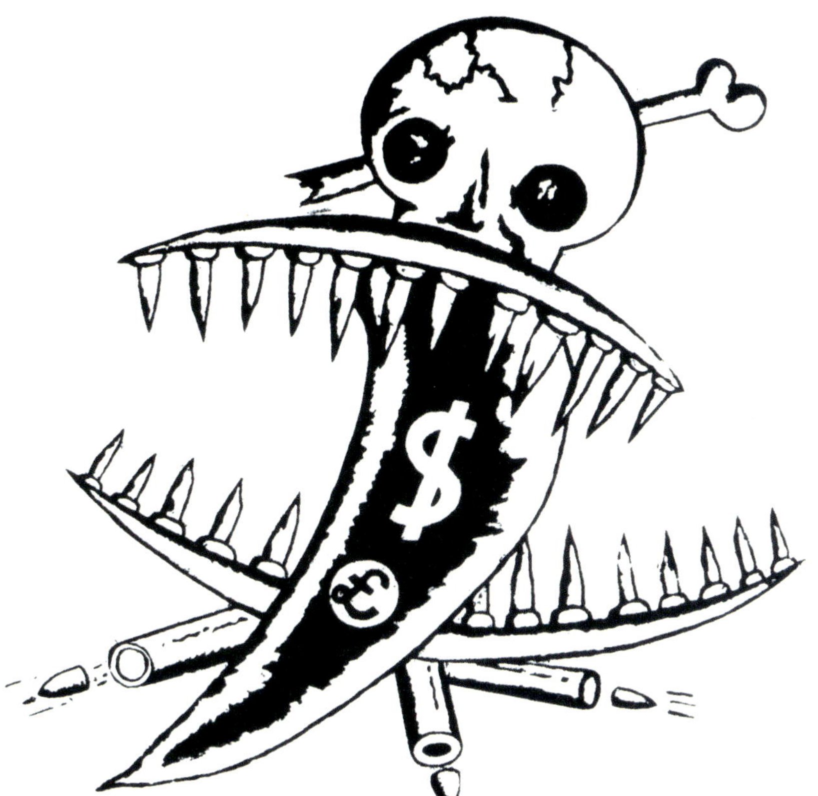

Vietnam

The Vietnam War had politicised a generation of radicals throughout the world. It was said that more bombs were dropped on Vietnam than on Europe in the Second World War, but this barbarous policy failed to 'bomb the Vietnamese people back to the stone age' as General Curtis LeMay had hoped – hence the outrage when *The Green Berets* film opened in Leicester Square. President Nixon was also met by protests when he visited London in February 1969.

Sam Lord and Nick Makepeace were arrested for carelessly fly posting the red *Thang Loi* sticker (p. 34) just as a police van was passing by. They were taken to Notting Hill police station. When Nick was asked for his name, he replied 'Nicholas Hartley'. The policeman turned to Sam and asked him for his name, at which point Nick interjected 'Makepeace'. Violence was only just avoided when Sam shouted 'Makepeace is his name'.

After the Ventriloquist (p. 40) refers to the 1968 Presidential election when Richard Nixon beat the vice-President Hubert Humphrey. Nixon, who had been a stalwart of the anti-Communist crusade in the 1950s, finally ended US efforts to defeat Vietnam in 1973. He was the only US President to have resigned from office (over the Watergate affair in 1974).

No Greeks in Vietnam (p. 33) was made by Australian Greeks – Greece itself was not involved in the war – but Australia was. Melbourne had the largest population of Greeks after Athens. *One Man One Rifle* (p. 34) was not intended as an advertisement for the National Rifle Association in America, but was probably meant to proclaim that peasant armies, individually armed, could defeat a mighty world power.

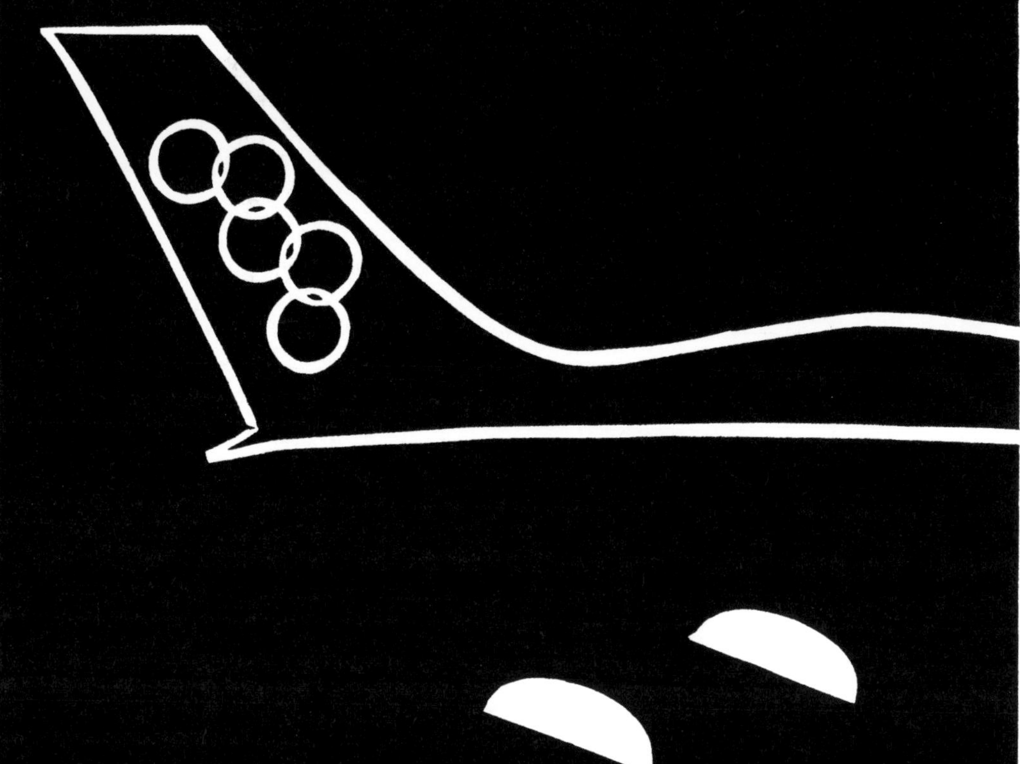

NO   GREEKS
IN VIET NAM

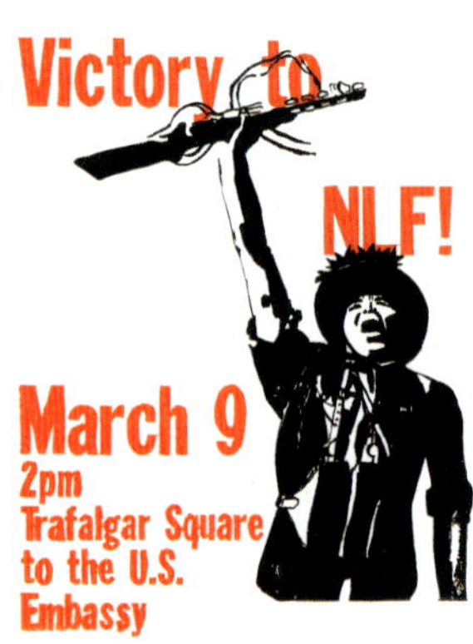
Victory to
NLF!
March 9
2pm
Trafalgar Square
to the U.S.
Embassy

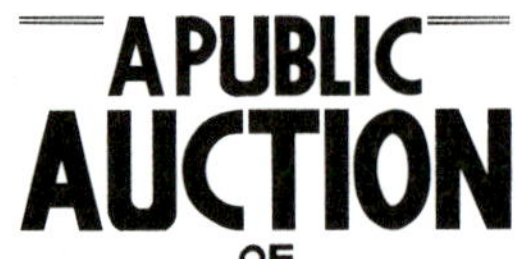
A PUBLIC
AUCTION
OF
THE BRITISH ISLES
a valuable property including
54 mill. inhabitants
WILL BE HELD AT
10 DOWNING St. on 25TH FEB.'69
CAN YOU OUTBID
PRESIDENT
RICHARD M. NIXON?
WILSON, HEATH, THORPE & Co.
AUCTIONEERS

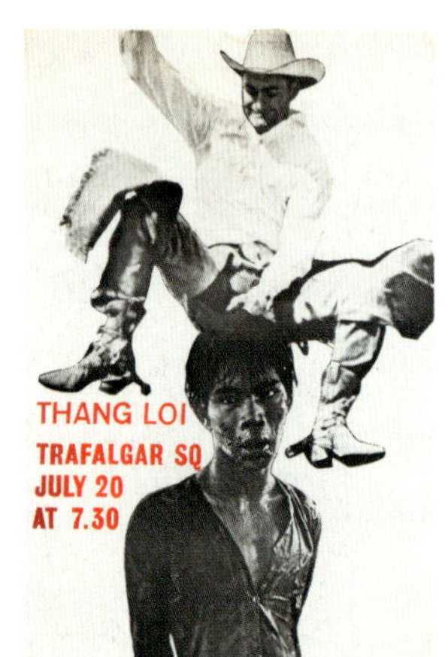
THANG LOI
TRAFALGAR SQ
JULY 20
AT 7.30

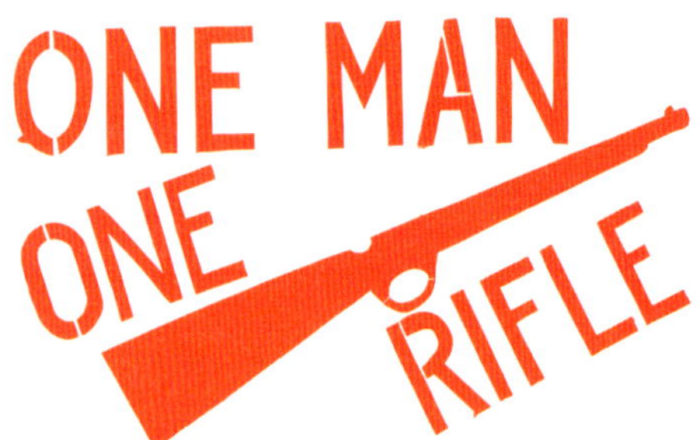
ONE MAN
ONE RIFLE

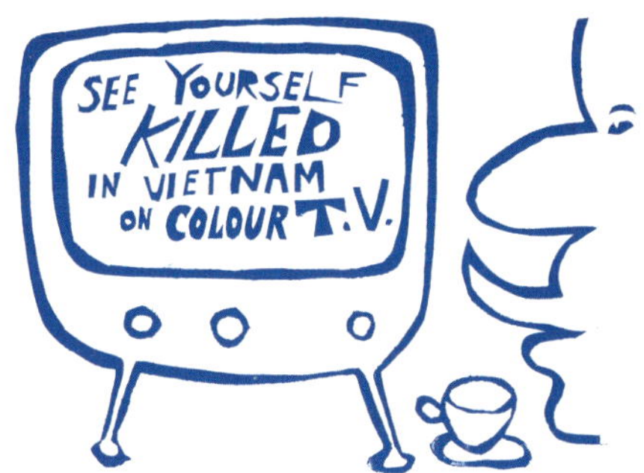
SEE YOURSELF
KILLED
IN VIETNAM
ON COLOUR T.V.

THANG LOI
TRAFALGAR SQ
JULY 20
AT 7.30
By courtesy of Abu
and the Tribune.

A MEETING OF AMERICAN RADICALS THE BRITISH SCENE WHERE IT'S AT

MONDAY OCT. 7TH 7:30 P.M.

CONWAY HALL, RED LION SQ. W.C.1

THE STOP-IT COMMITTEE   59 FLEET ST. E.C. 4

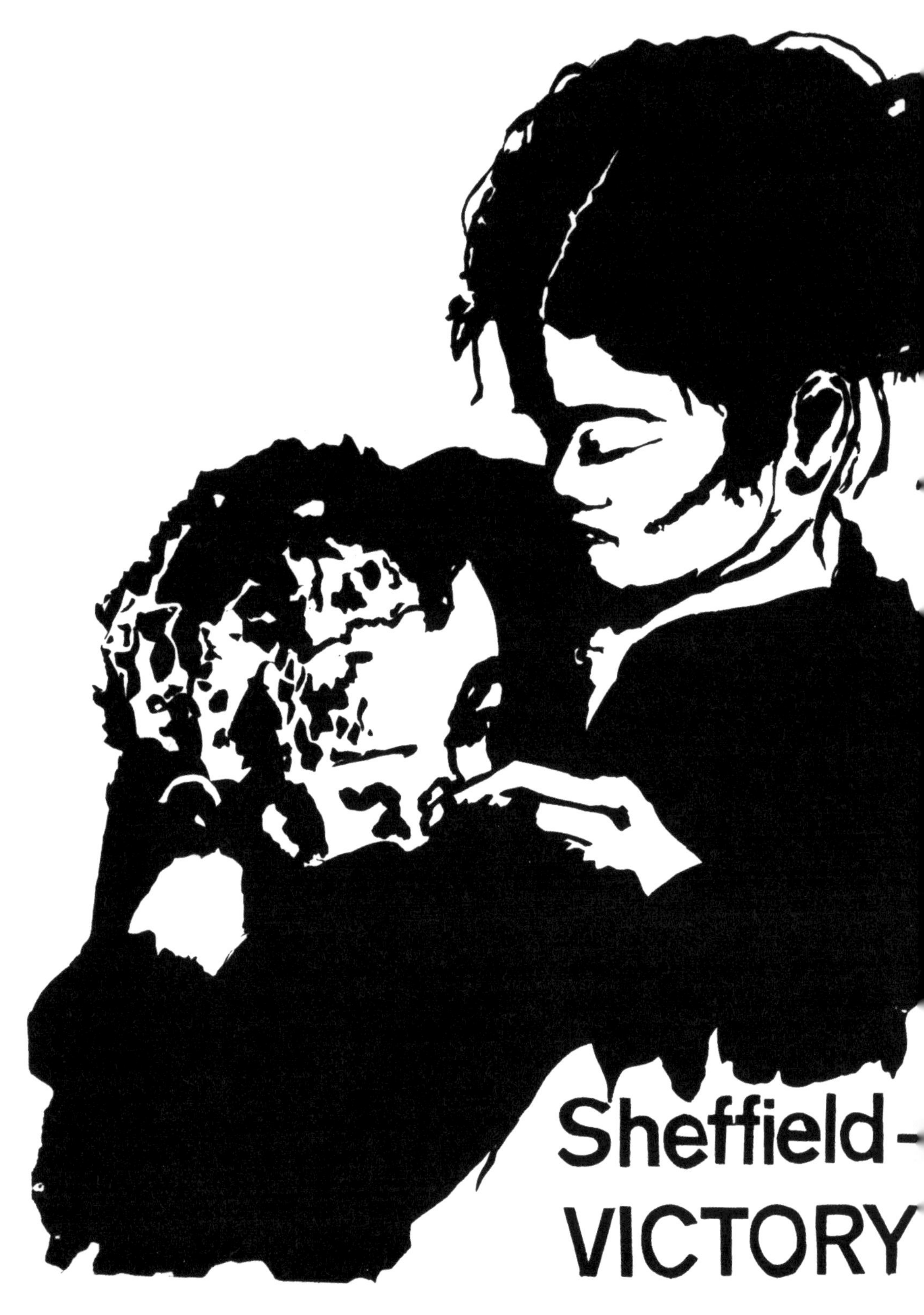

Sheffield -
VICTORY

SHEFFIELD VIETNAM DEMONSTRATION

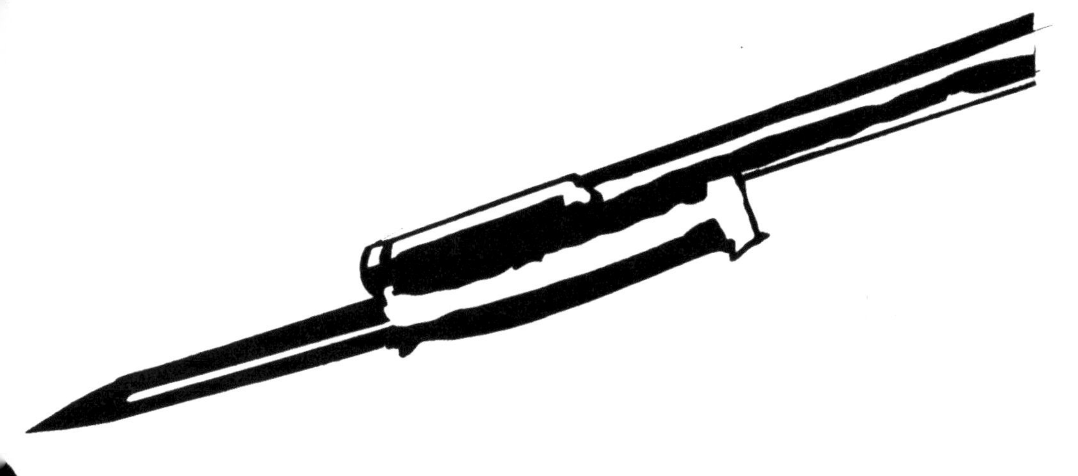

2pm Sat March 1st
to Sheffield City Hall
assemble Tinsley Wire
nsley turn-off from M1
PEACE IN VIETNAM

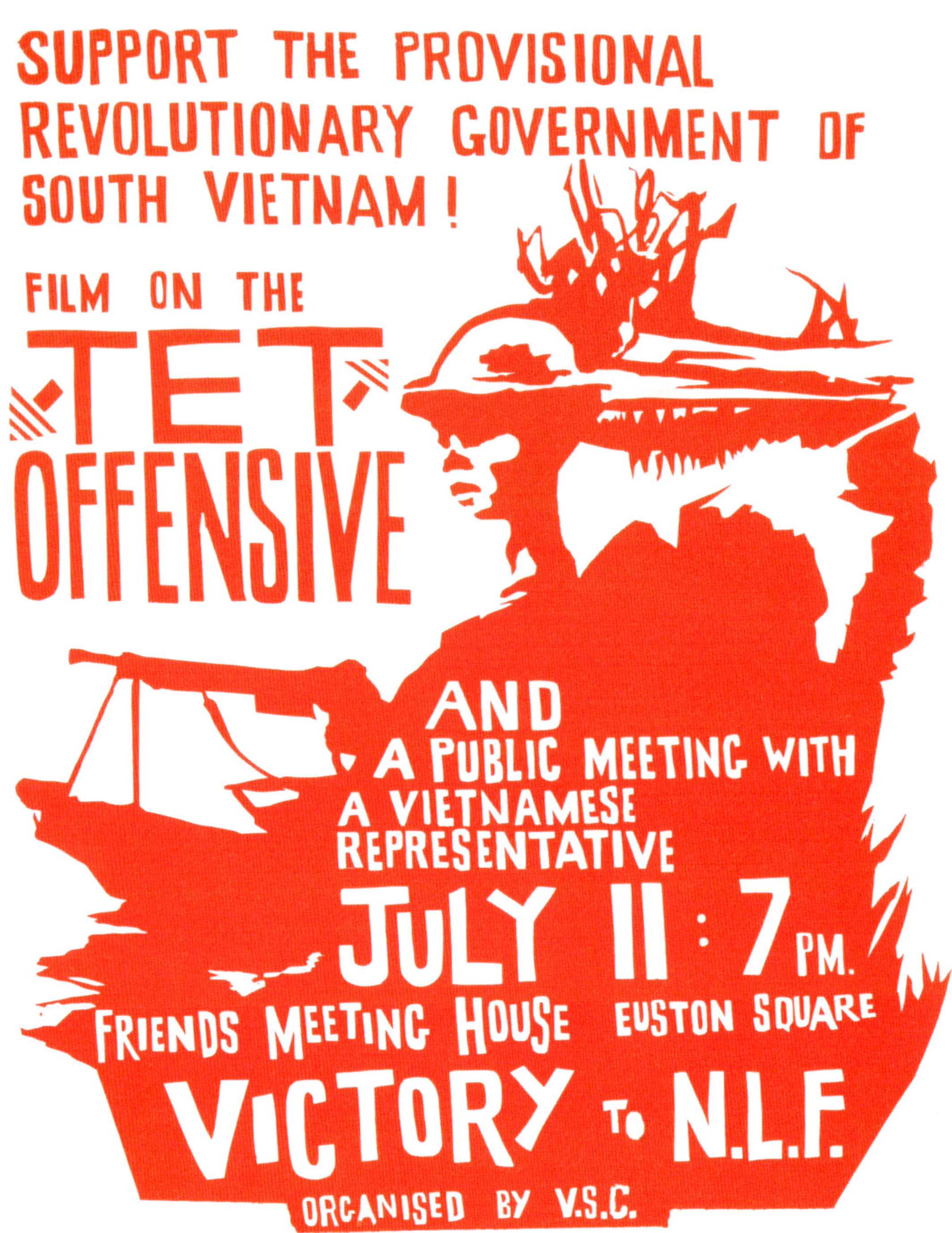

SUPPORT THE PROVISIONAL REVOLUTIONARY GOVERNMENT OF SOUTH VIETNAM!
FILM ON THE
'TET' OFFENSIVE
AND
A PUBLIC MEETING WITH
A VIETNAMESE
REPRESENTATIVE
JULY 11 : 7 PM.
FRIENDS MEETING HOUSE   EUSTON SQUARE
VICTORY TO N.L.F.
ORGANISED BY V.S.C.

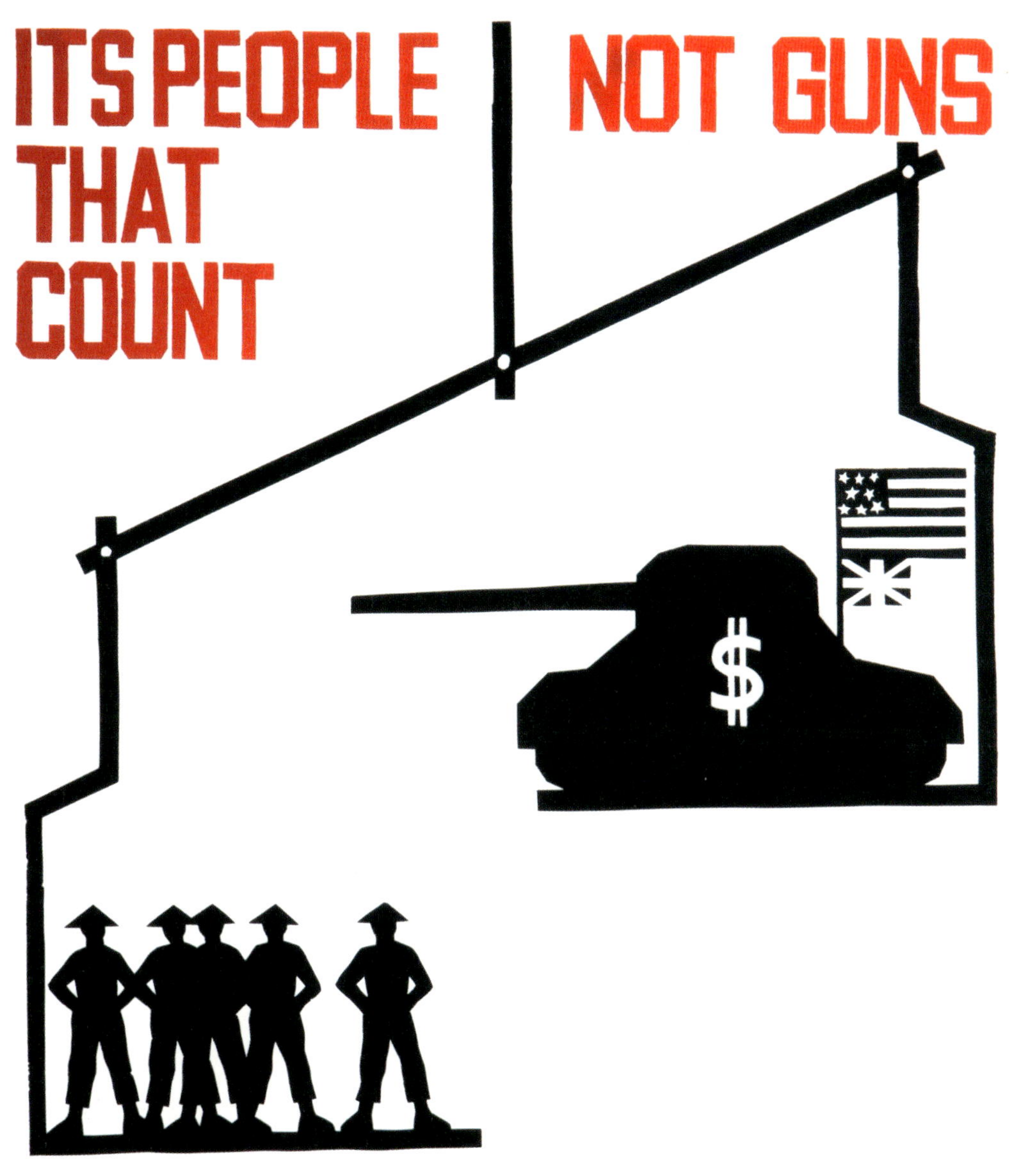

ITS PEOPLE THAT COUNT
NOT GUNS
$
THE NATIONAL LIBERATION FRONT IS THE PEOPLE OF VIETNAM

NLF NLF NLF
WIN WIN WIN

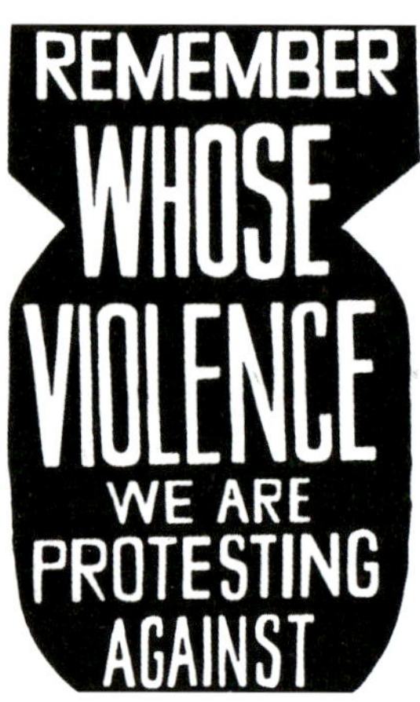

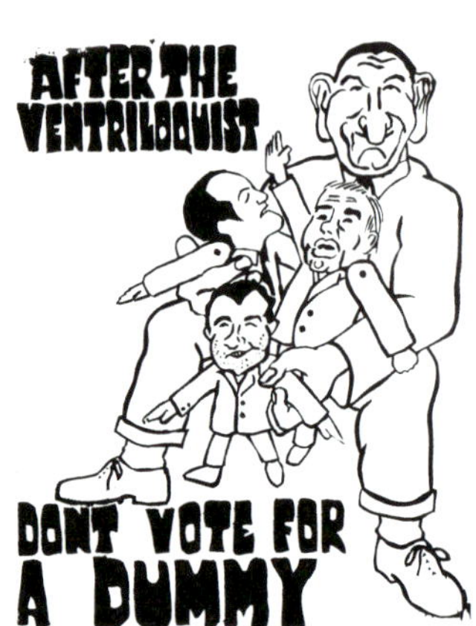

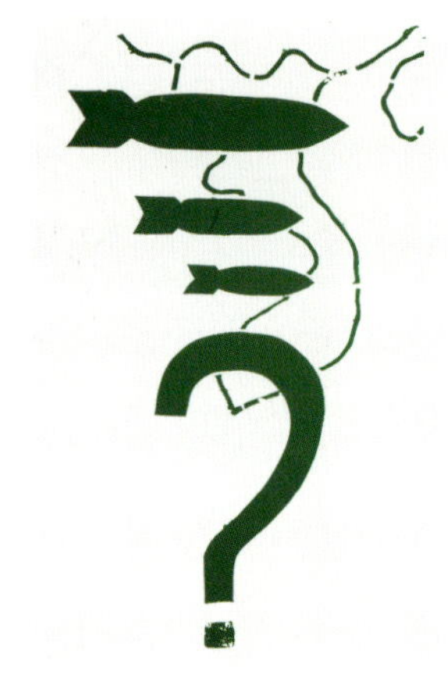

THE N.L.F. ARE
WINNING THEIR
FIGHT IN VIETNAM

WHAT IS OUR
FIGHT ?

U.K.

51st.

STATE

OF

U.S.

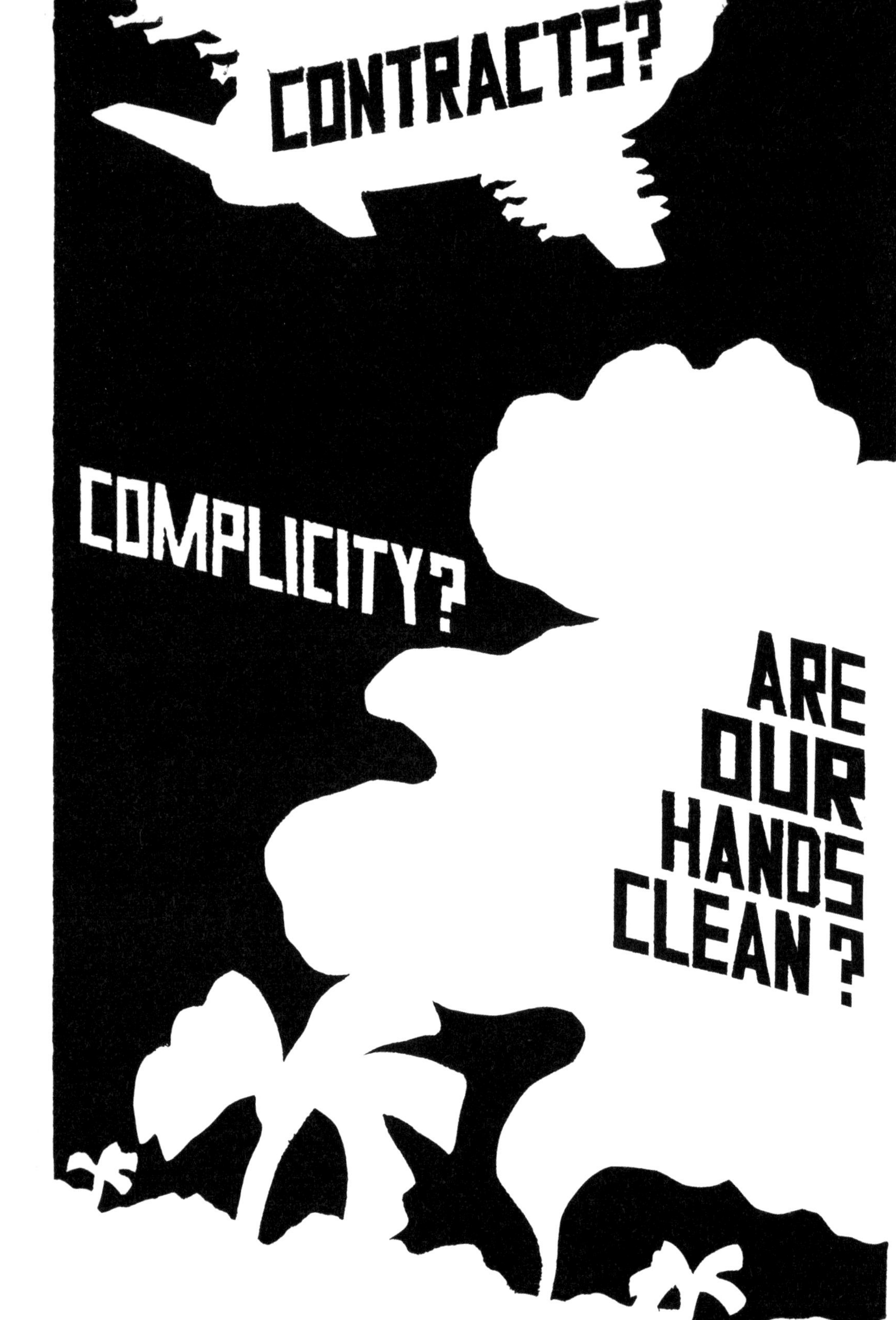

CONTRACTS?
COMPLICITY?
ARE
OUR
HANDS
CLEAN ?

THE GREEN BERETS

WITH **JOHN WAYNE** AND CO-STARRING

THE DEAD VIETNAMESE PEOPLE

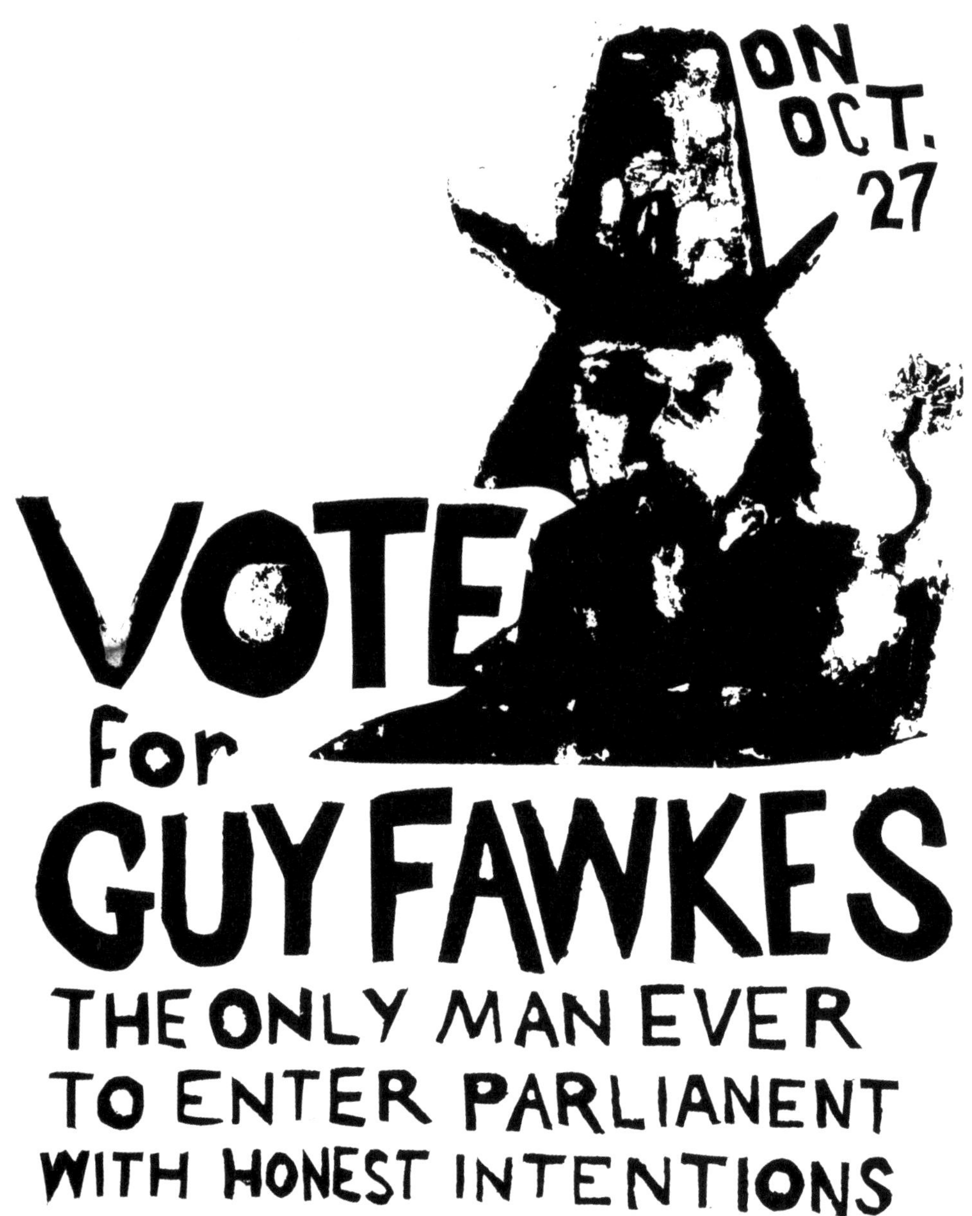

ON OCT. 27
VOTE FOR GUY FAWKES
THE ONLY MAN EVER
TO ENTER PARLIANENT
WITH HONEST INTENTIONS

LET'S GIVE
NIXON A
HOT
RECEPTION
FEB. 24-28

In 1967 the Students Union at the London School of Economics held a sit-in protesting the appointment of Walter Adams as Director. He had previously worked in Rhodesia Now Zimbabwe and was accused of complicity with Ian Smith's racist regime. Fearing that the Vietnam demonstration on 27 October 1968 would lead to a student occupation of the LSE, Adams arranged for the gates to be locked. Students broke down the seven protective gates with sledge hammers and occupied the building between 24 and 27 October. The Poster Workshop were invited to join the fun. *The Economic Facts* (p. 57) outlines the corporate and vested interests of the Governors which the students were rebelling against.

Adams Provokes Direct Action (p. 54) was printed co-opting the image on a donated poster. *Education for Death* (p. 47) was a protest against institutionalised recruitment for the Armed Forces taking place in Universities.

Militant school pupils formed the 'Schools Action Union' in January 1969 to campaign for a true comprehensive education system (p. 60). Two posters were made to advertise the Living School, a radical student-led form of education, at the LSE, *Down wiv Skool* (p. 61) and *Living School* (p. 59) which was printed by pupils from Camden School for Girls. (*The Little Red School Book* was published in 1969 by Danish Educationalists, Soren Hansen and Jesper Jensen to demystify Education, sex and drugs. So much scandal! It was prosecuted under the Obscene Publications Act. Soren says that although authoritarianism is now reduced, children suffer more today in the dog-eat-dog competition that has replaced it.) Corporal punishment was not abolished in English schools until 1986, and in private schools until 1999.

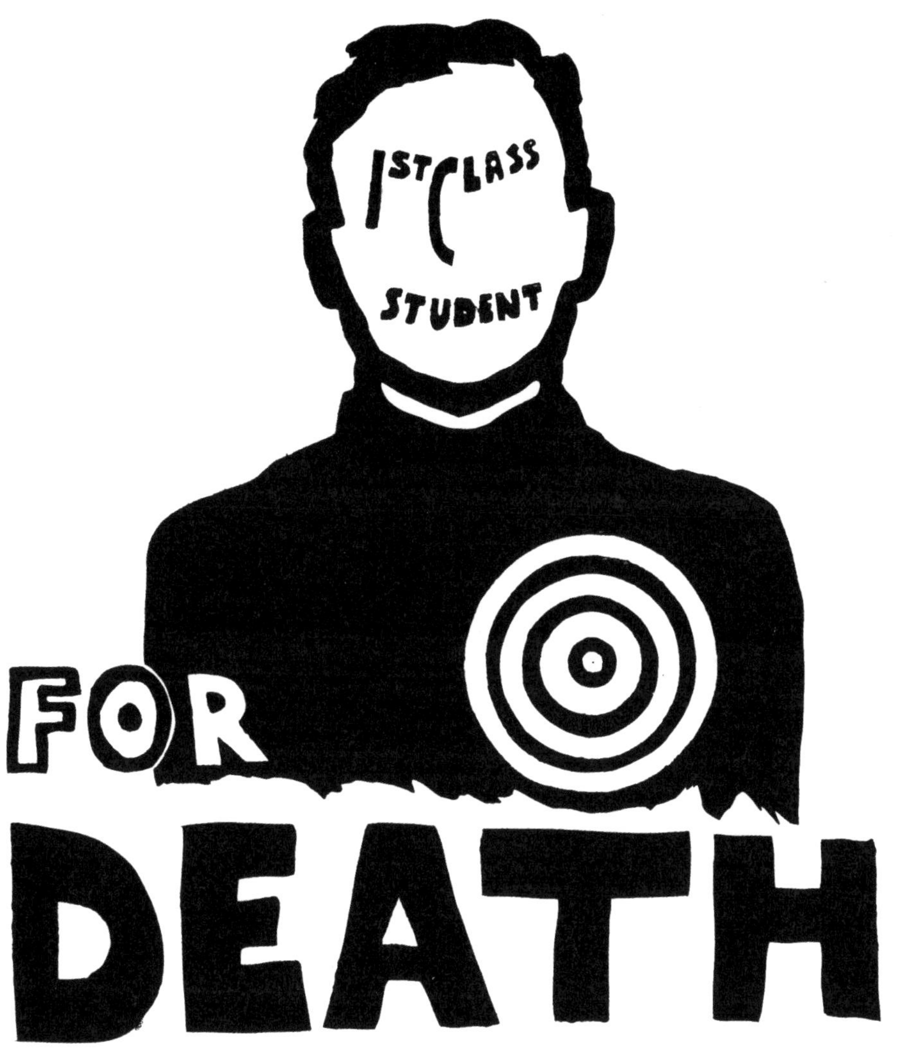

EDUCATION
1st CLASS STUDENT
FOR
DEATH

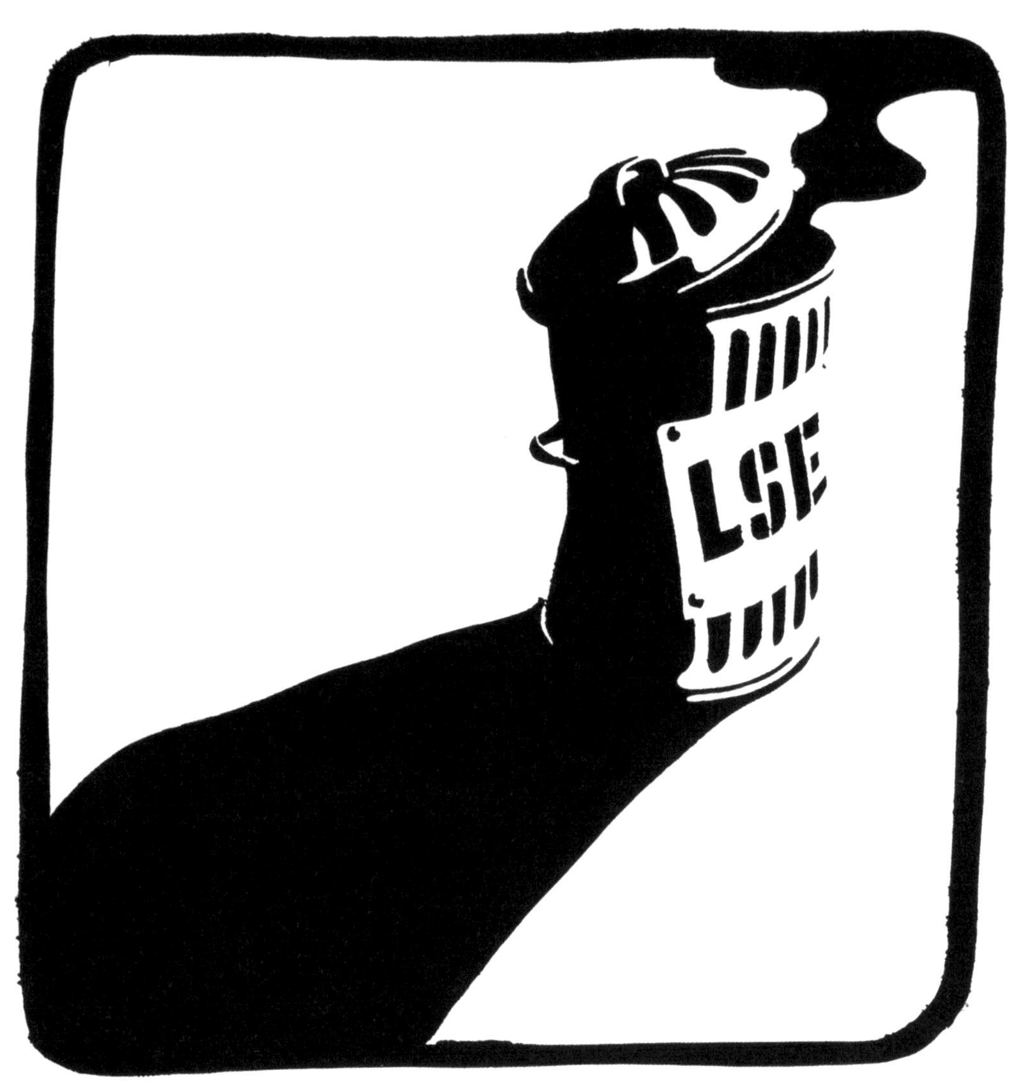

TOWARDS THE INCINERATION OF ACADEMIC MYSTOLOGY !!

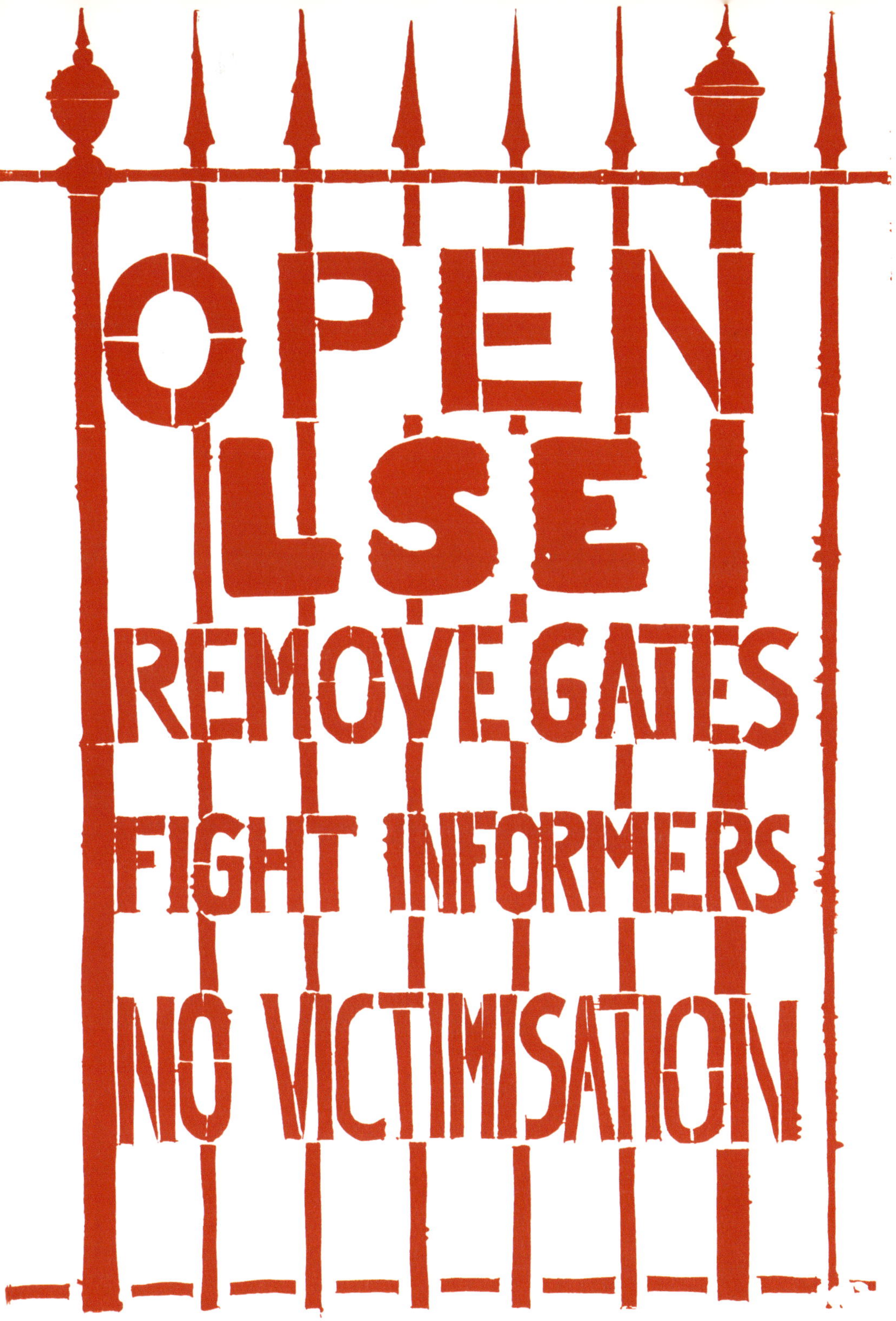

OPEN
LSE
REMOVE GATES
FIGHT INFORMERS
NO VICTIMISATION

ADMINISTRATION BEATS UP 1 STUDENT

ADMINISTRATION + POLICE ARREST 5

ADMINISTRATION + POLICE + "JUSTICE"
WILL GAOL 5

FOR FUCKS SAKE
DO SOMETHING

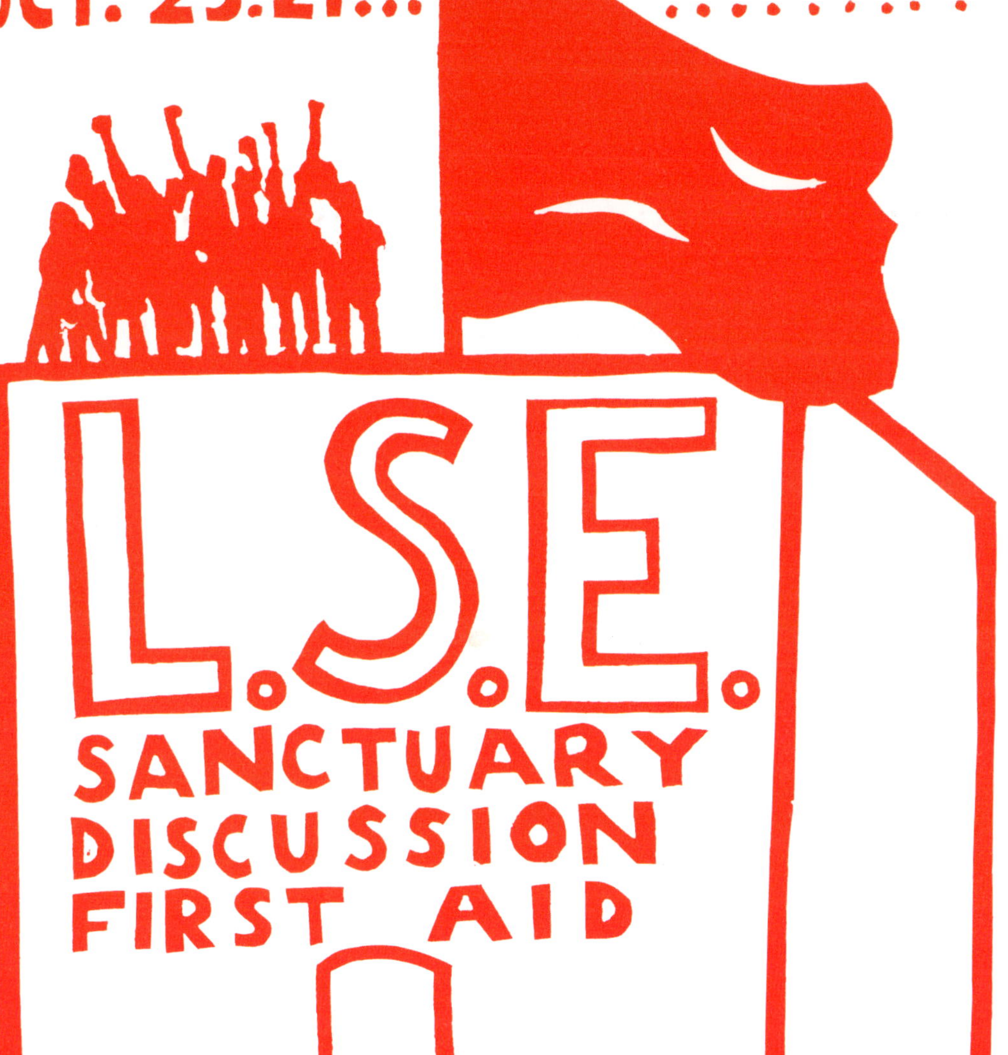

OCCUPIED
OCT. 25. 27... ....
L.S.E.
SANCTUARY
DISCUSSION
FIRST AID

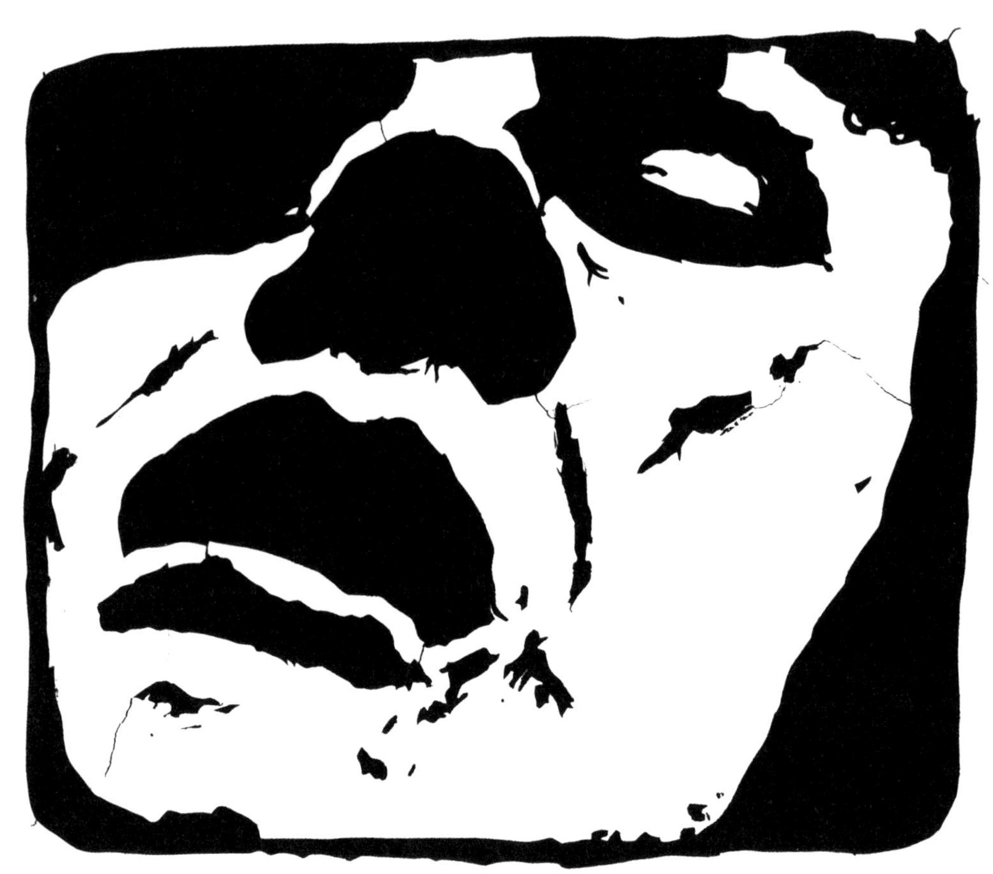

THEY'VE CLOSED THE
SORBONNE MADRID
BERLIN LAW FACULTY
HORNSEY COLUMBIA
MEXICO TOKYO
GUILDFORD AND NOW
LSE - SOLIDARITY
WITH LSE STUDENTS

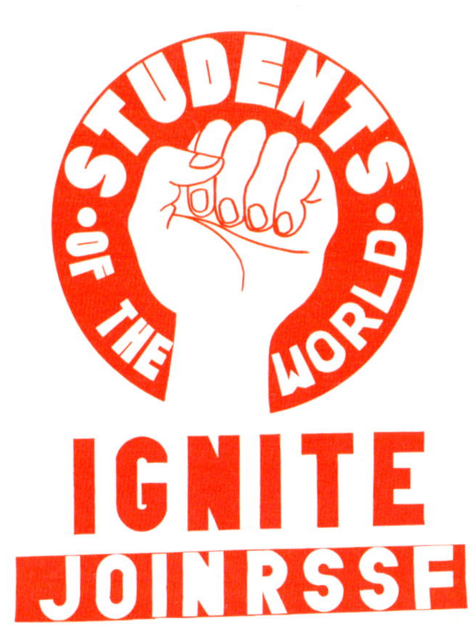

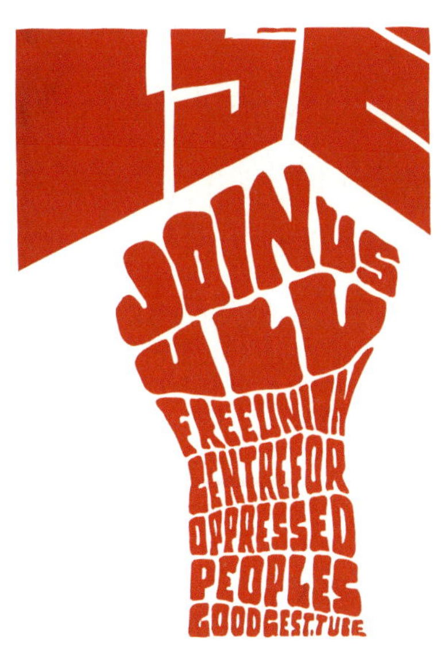

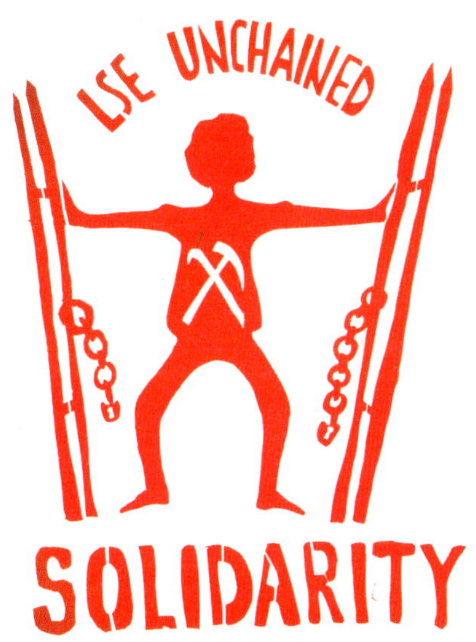

WHY WASTE THE
TAX PAYERS
MONEY ON BLOODY
LSE STUDENTS?

WE ARE WASTING THE
TAX PAYERS MONEY
LEARNING HOW TO
WASTE THE TAX
PAYERS MONEY

£ 3½ MILLION ON
NEW KENSINGTON
TOWN HALL
WHILE 16000
HOMELESS

END WASTE &
FREE LSE —
DESTROY CAPITALISM

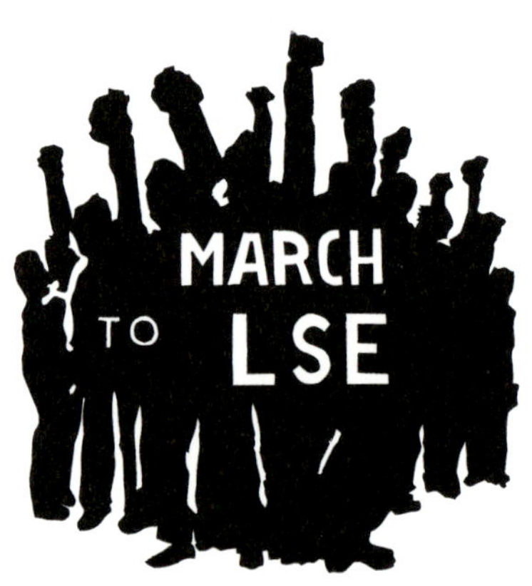

THURS JAN 30
6.30 FROM U.L.U.
(MALET ST.)

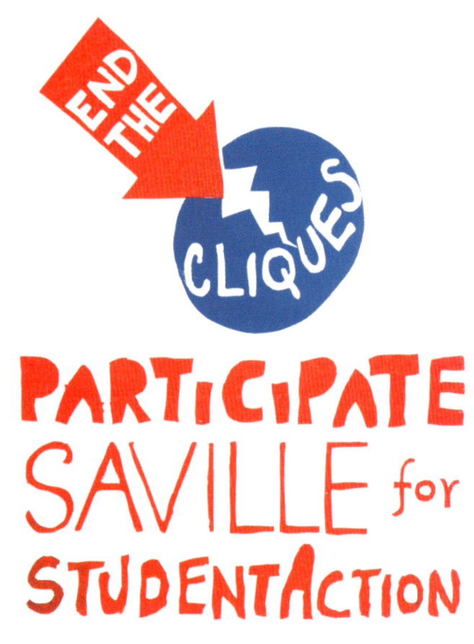

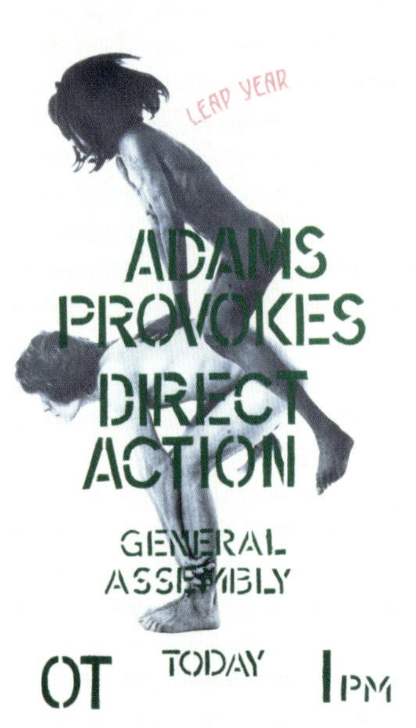

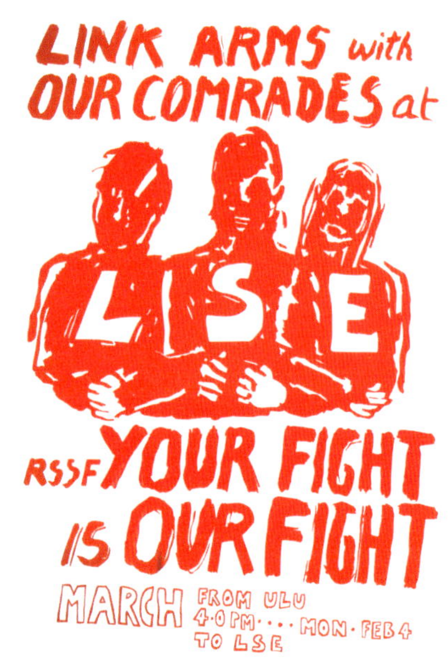

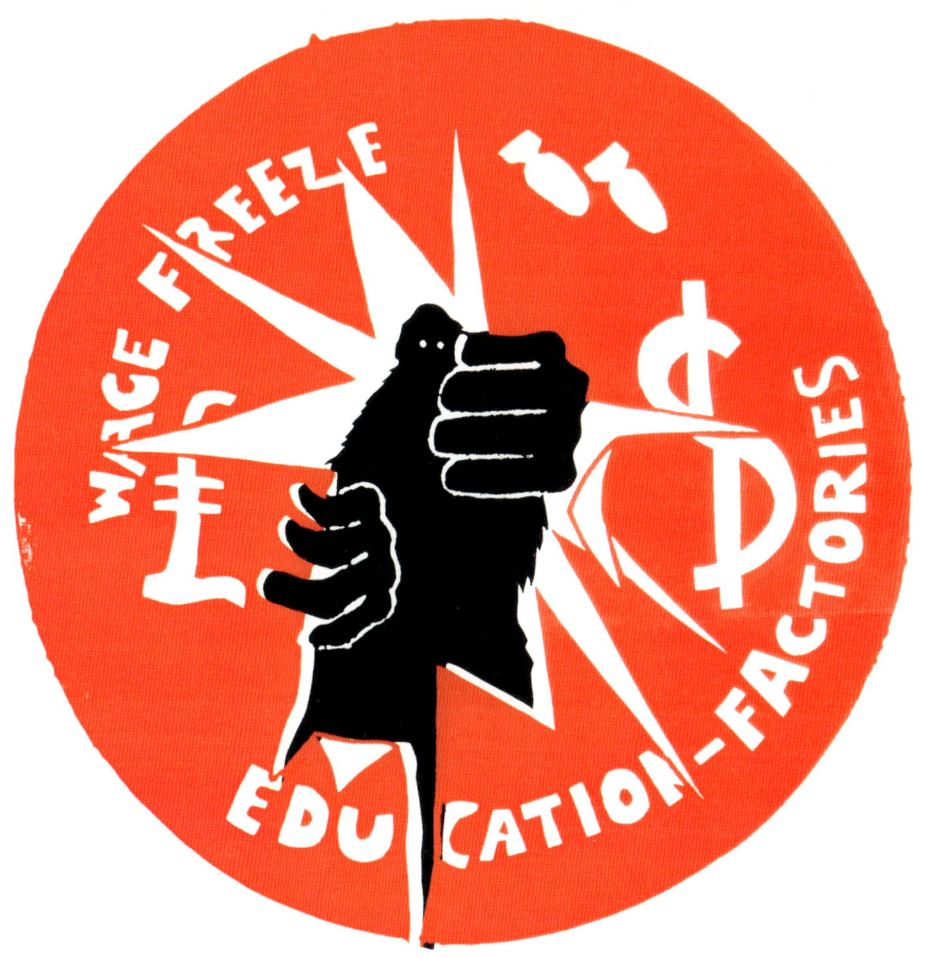

"GORILLA"
WAGE FREEZE
£
EDUCATION-FACTORIES
BREAKS LOOSE
ON WEDNESDAY
BRUNEL. EALING TECH. CHISWICK POLY.
MANRESA
READ GORILLA 6.

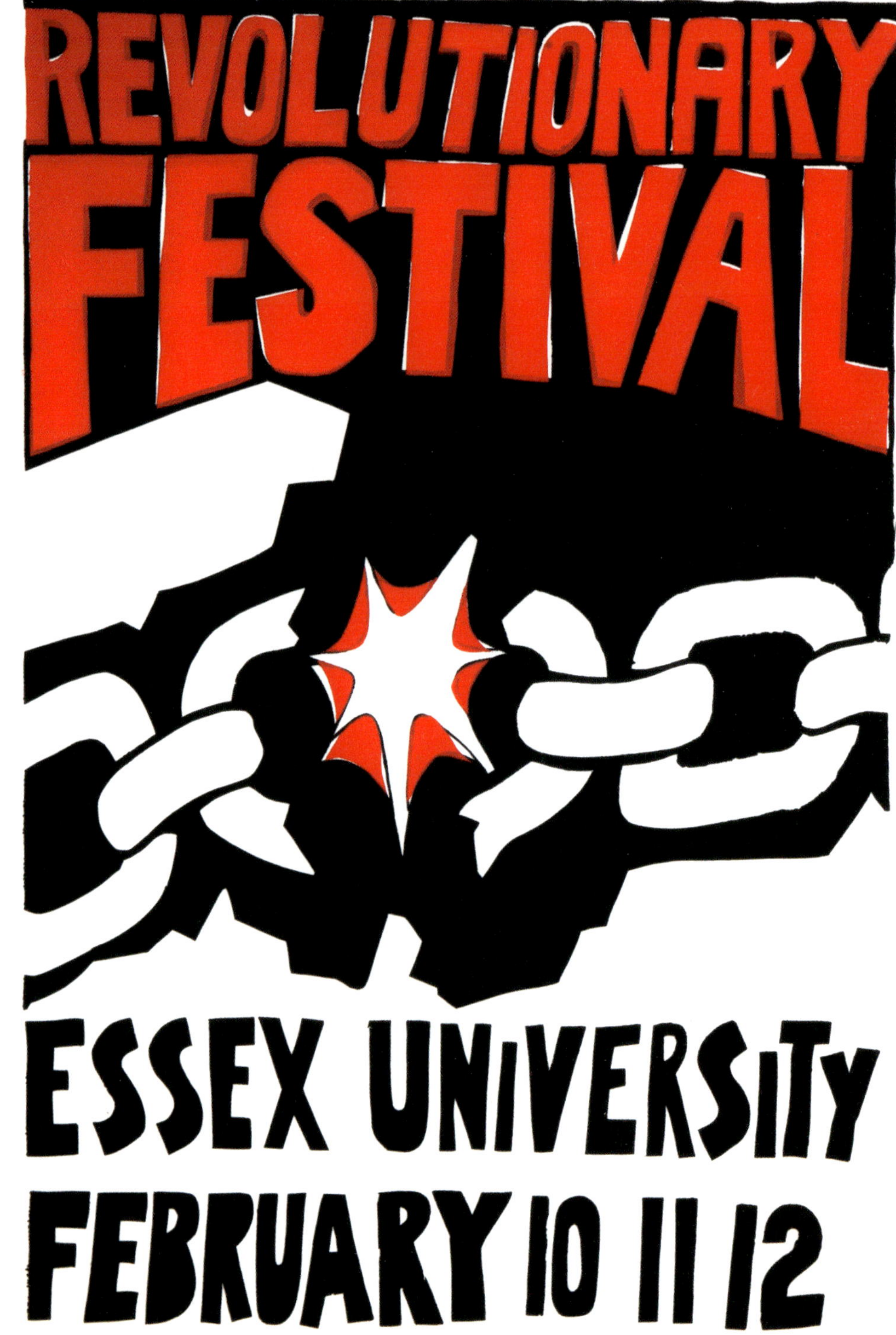

REVOLUTIONARY
FESTIVAL
ESSEX UNIVERSITY
FEBRUARY 10 11 12

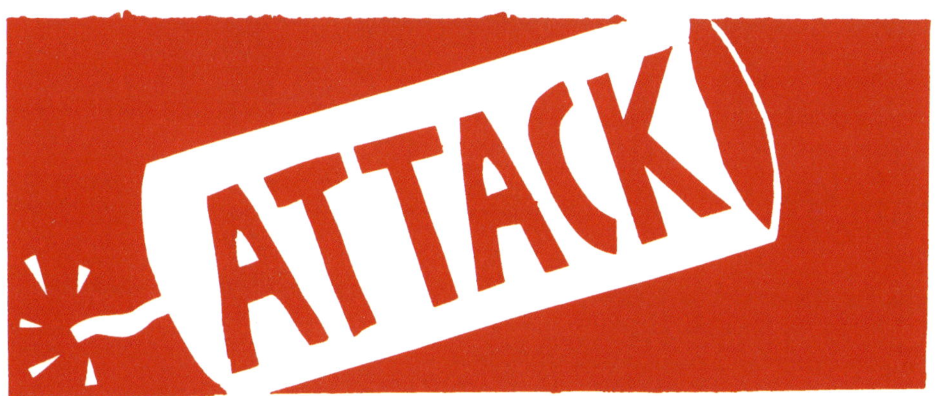

ECONOMIC FACTS
SOUTH AFRICA
RHODESIA
$
BP
DE BEERS
ICI
AEI
UNILEVER
£
UNION MINING CORPORATION
LSE GOVERNORS
ATTACK!

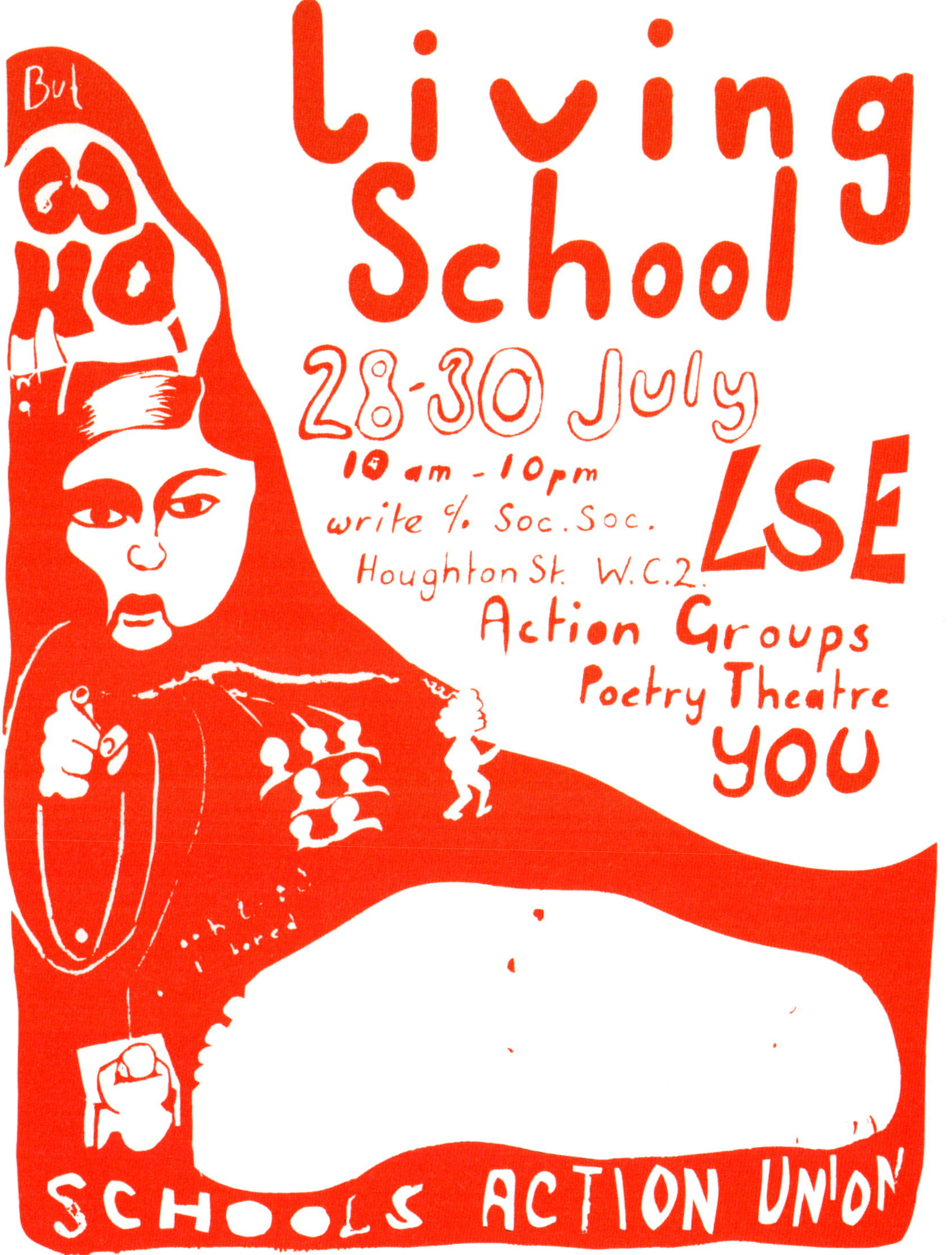
But
3 Ho,
Living School
28-30 July
10 am - 10pm
write % Soc. Soc.
Houghton St. W.C.2.
LSE
Action Groups
Poetry Theatre
YOU
SCHOOLS ACTION UNION

SchoolsActionUnion

★ student & staff control ★ coed comprehensive ed.

★ freedom of speech & assembly ★ more pay for teachers

★ outlaw corporal punishment ★ abolition of school uniforms

demonstrate for your rights

2 p.m. Sunday March 2nd.

march from speakers corner to county hall

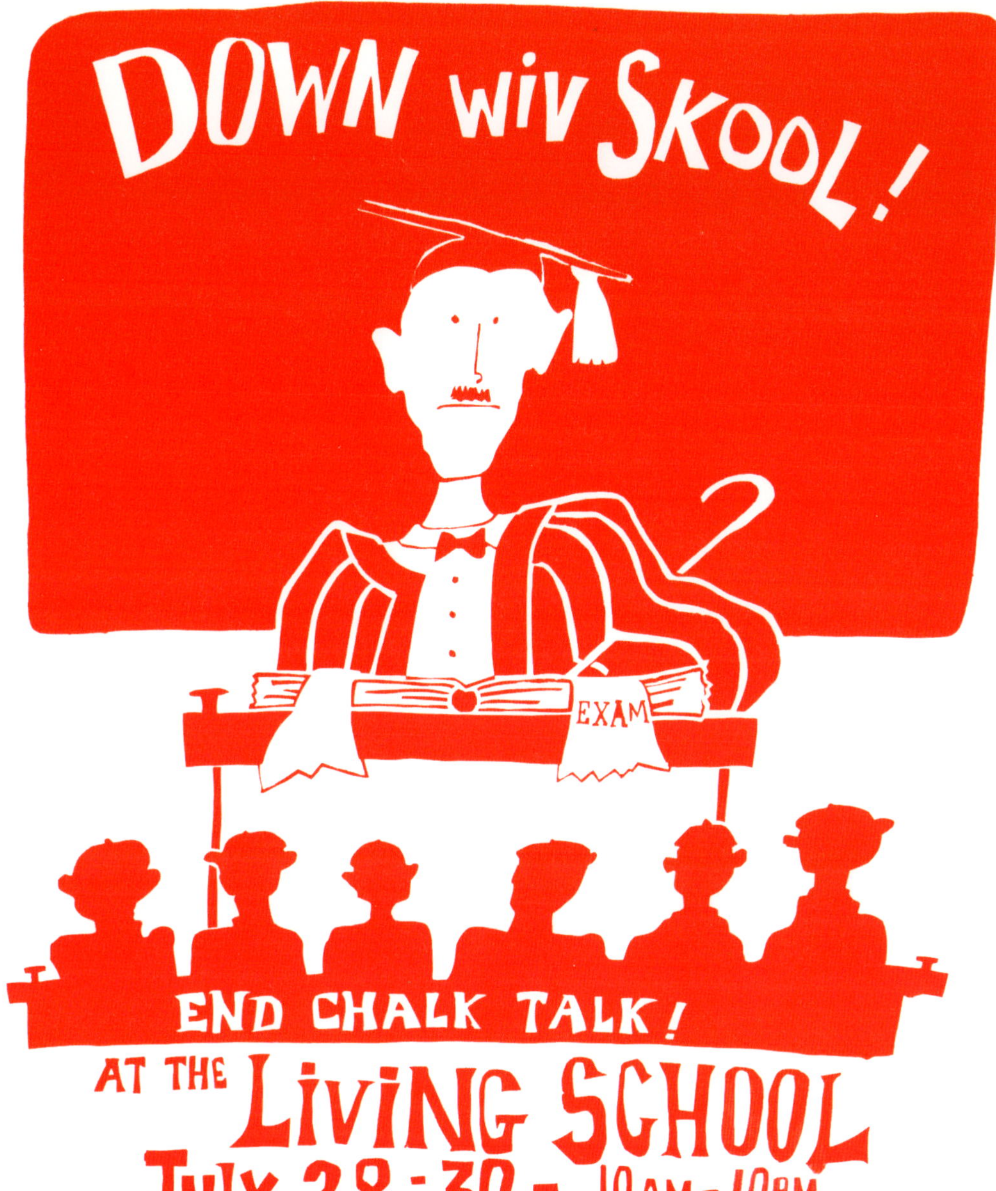

DOWN wiv SKOOL!
EXAM
END CHALK TALK!
AT THE LIVING SCHOOL
July 28 - 30 - 10AM - 10PM
L.S.E. HOUGHTON ST. WC 2 - CONTACT - SOC-SOC
ACTION - DISCUSSION - GROUPS
POETRY - THEATRE

Workers Control (p. 63) and *Same Bosses Same Fight* (p. 71) were printed at the LSE during the student occupation in October 1968.

In 1966 the Labour Government had to devalue the currency, but the fragile economy did not recover. Unions became more militant. In 1969, Prime Minister Harold Wilson and his Secretary of State for Employment and Productivity, Barbara Castle, together cooked up a White Paper, 'In Place of Strife', in an attempt to curb the power of the Trades Unions. They sprang this on the Cabinet who were deeply divided. There was such strong opposition – *Scrap the White Paper* (p. 72), *Cooking with Barbara* (p. 66), *A Spoonful of Sugar* (p. 68) and *All Out May Day* (p. 64) – that the proposals were dropped. Although the legislation was shelved, the requirement that strike action could only take place after a ballot of Trade Union members, ironically became the route for Mrs Thatcher's assault on the unions years later. It divided the Labour Party and alienated local parties from the centre.

Mass Meeting and *Strike Meeting* (p. 64) were posters made for shop stewards at Ford in Dagenham.

Days Lost (p. 64) illustrates the startling amount of working time lost through accidents and sickness in a time before Health and Safety. *The Royal Group Docks Campaign* (p. 72), led by veteran Communist Trade Unionist, Jack Dash, managed to triple dockers' wages between 1959 and 1972. On 22 October 1968, dockers marched on Parliament in support of Enoch Powell's anti-immigration policy. The dockers were to be swept away by containerisation in the 1970s.

The Boss Needs You (p. 72) was a direct translation of a poster from the Atelier Populaire.

The Punfield and Barstow strike in 1968, at the Queensbury Industrial Estate, Middlesex, was predominantly made up of poorly paid immigrant workers fighting for better conditions and a guaranteed bonus (p. 64).

Support Upper Clyde Workers (p. 73) backed the ship builders who, in an attempt to prevent closure, eventually occupied and ran a work-in at the UCS shipyard in 1971 under the inspiring leadership of Jimmy Reid. The work-in gained massive popular support. Prime Minister Ted Heath was forced to temporarily back down and UCS stayed in business. Despite a full order book, the Conservative Government refused to lend any money and UCS collapsed in 1972.

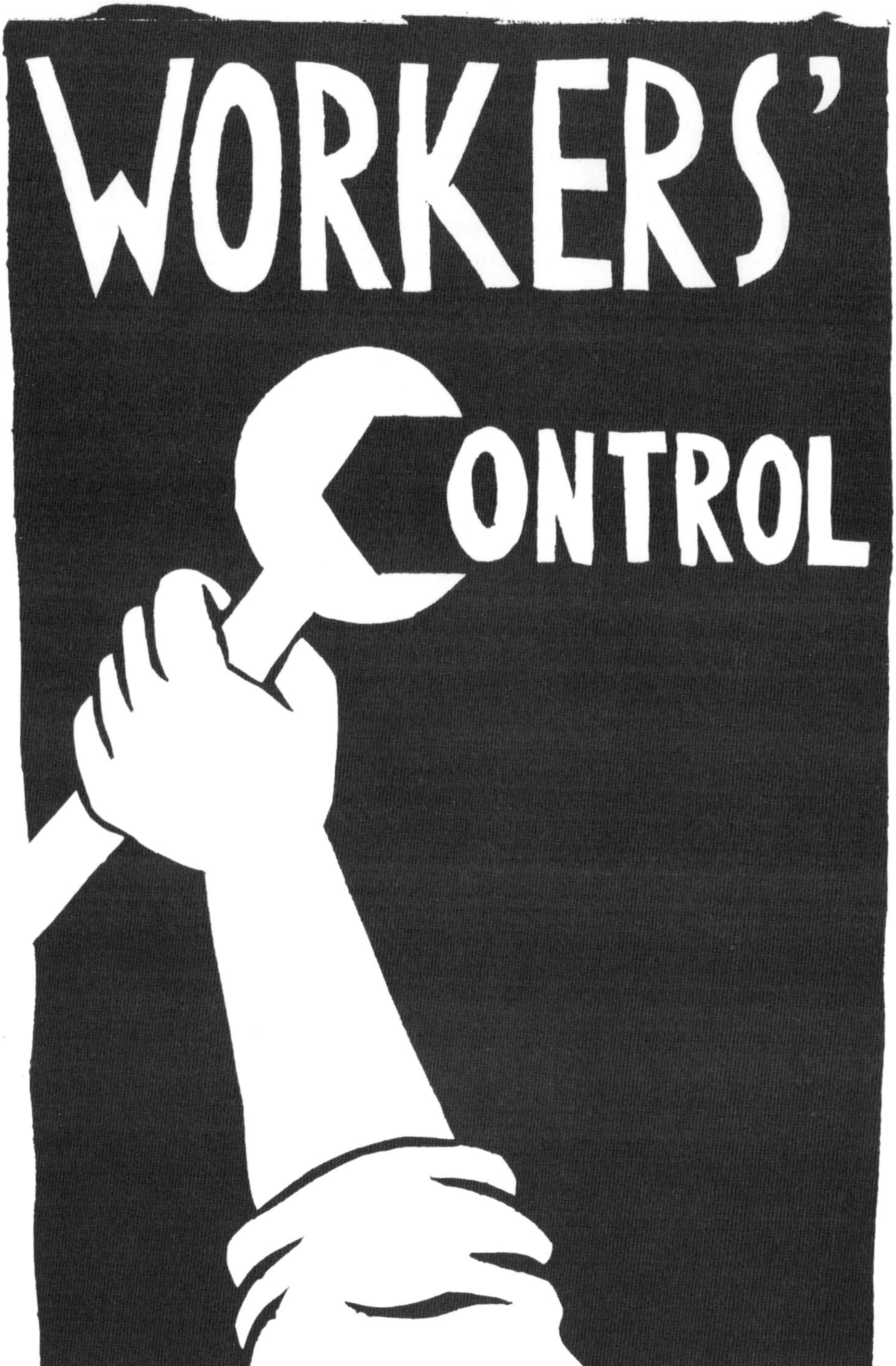

WORKERS'
CONTROL

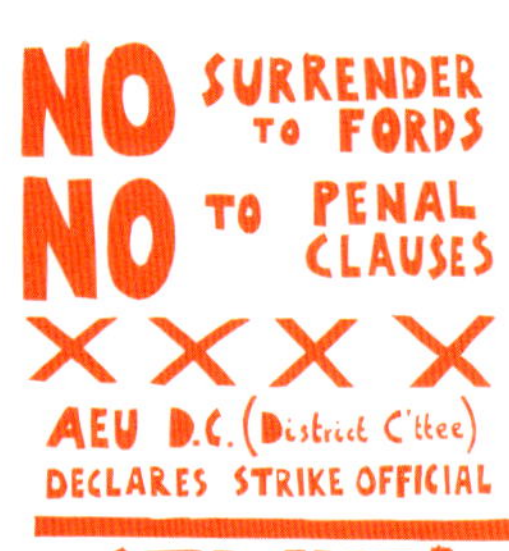

NO SURRENDER TO FORDS
NO TO PENAL CLAUSES
X X X X
AEU D.C. (District C'ttee)
DECLARES STRIKE OFFICIAL
STRIKE!
FOR BETTER PAY
FOR FORD WORKERS

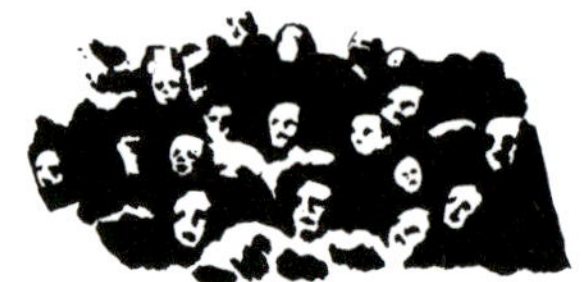

ALL OUT MAY DAY
SMASH THE WHITE PAPER

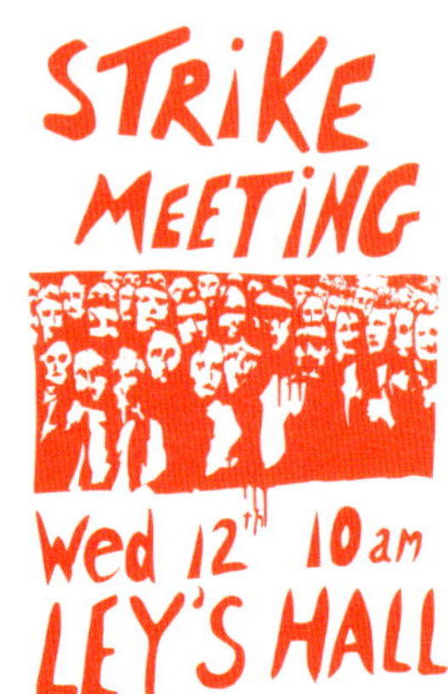

STRIKE MEETING
Wed 12th 10am
LEY'S HALL

DAYS LOST THROUGH
LOCK-OUTS & STRIKES:
LESS THAN 5 MILL.
INFLUENZA: 13 MILL.
BRONCHITIS: 33 MILL.
ACCIDENTS: 43 MILL.
TOTAL BY ACCIDENTS &
SICKNESS: 311 MILL.

READ VOICE OF FORD WORKERS
HIGHEST PROFIT
LOWEST WAGES
HIGHEST PRODUCTIVITY
LOWEST EARNINGS
WAGE PARITY NOW

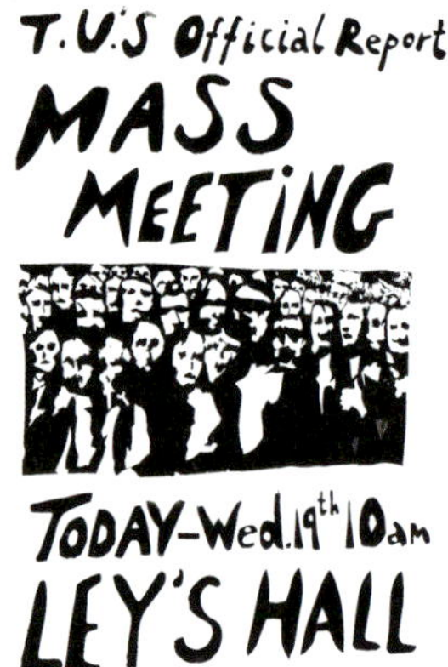

T.U.'s Official Report
MASS MEETING
TODAY—Wed. 19th 10am
LEY'S HALL

FORD WORKERS STRIKE
NOW OFFICIAL
DO NOT WORK AGAINST
UNIONS RECOMMENDATIONS
STRIKE NOW against PENAL CLAUSES
UNITY IS STRENGTH

SUPPORT THE NURSES' DEMONSTRATION
WE WANT:
A 40 HOUR WEEK
ON CALL PAYMENTS
DUTY ROTAS TO BE PLANNED
WELL AHEAD
UNPOPULAR HOURS FAIRLY SHARED
ESSENTIAL STUDY PERIODS TO BE
LONGER
NO VICTIMISATION
10.30 MEETING AT TOWER HILL
WEDNESDAY JUNE 18TH
MARCH VIA FLEET STREET
TO PARLIAMENT
nurses action group
c/o 23 Bromfield St N.I

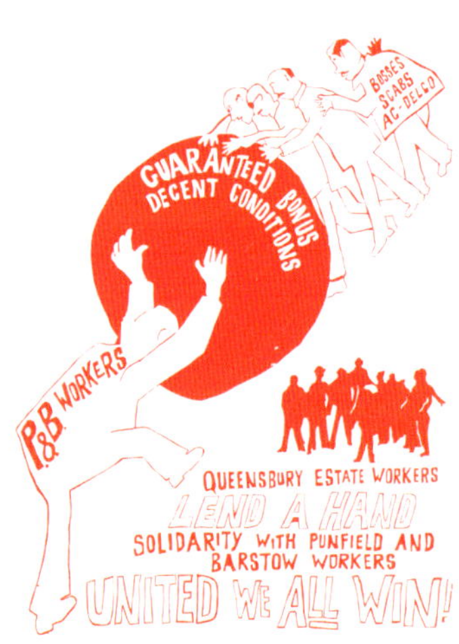

BOSSES SCABS AC-DELCO
GUARANTEED BONUS DECENT CONDITIONS
P&B WORKERS
QUEENSBURY ESTATE WORKERS
LEND A HAND
SOLIDARITY WITH PUNFIELD AND
BARSTOW WORKERS
UNITED WE ALL WIN!

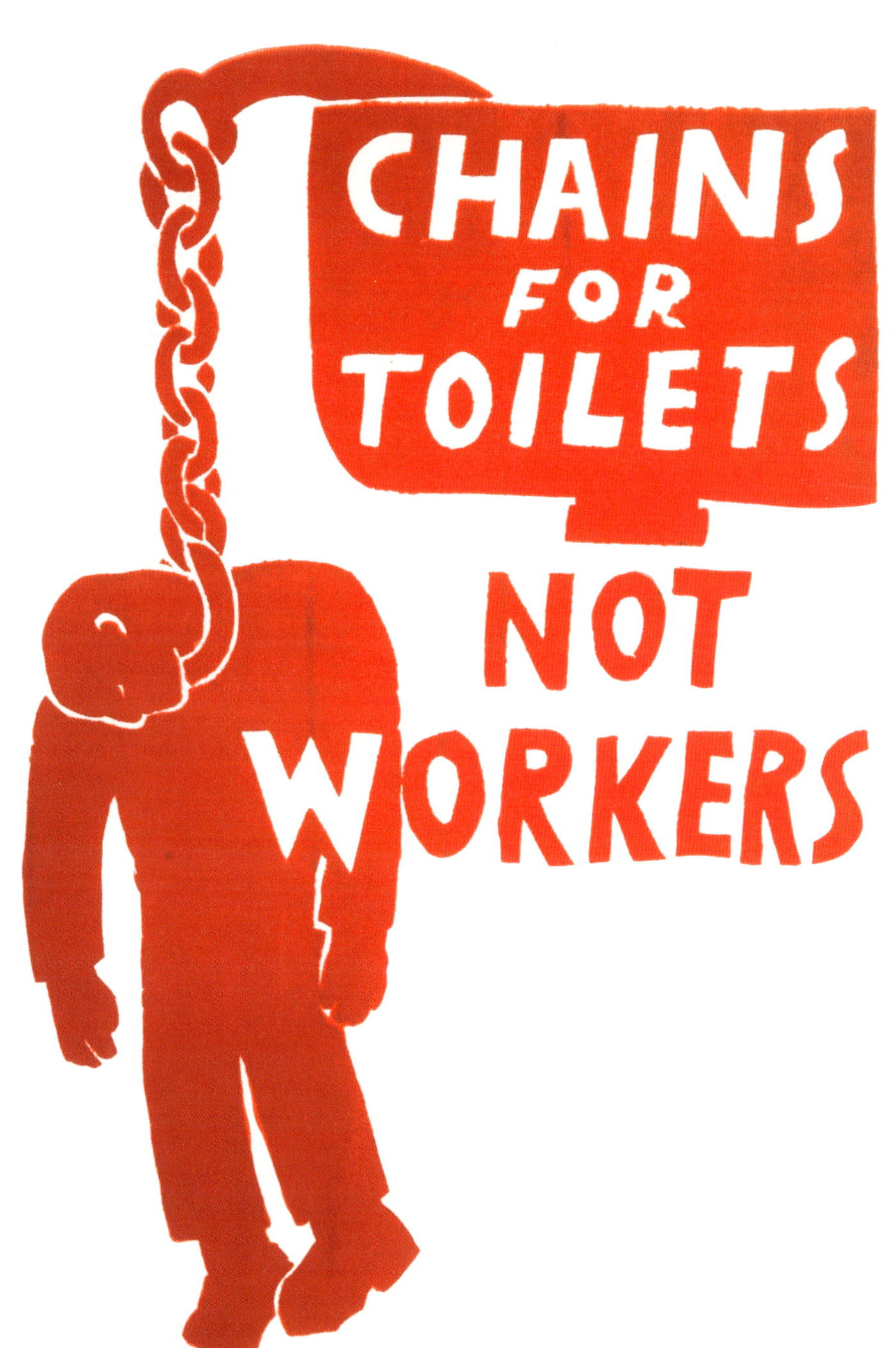

CHAINS
FOR
TOILETS
NOT
WORKERS

IN PLACE OF STRIFE
IT'S A PIECE OF CAKE!

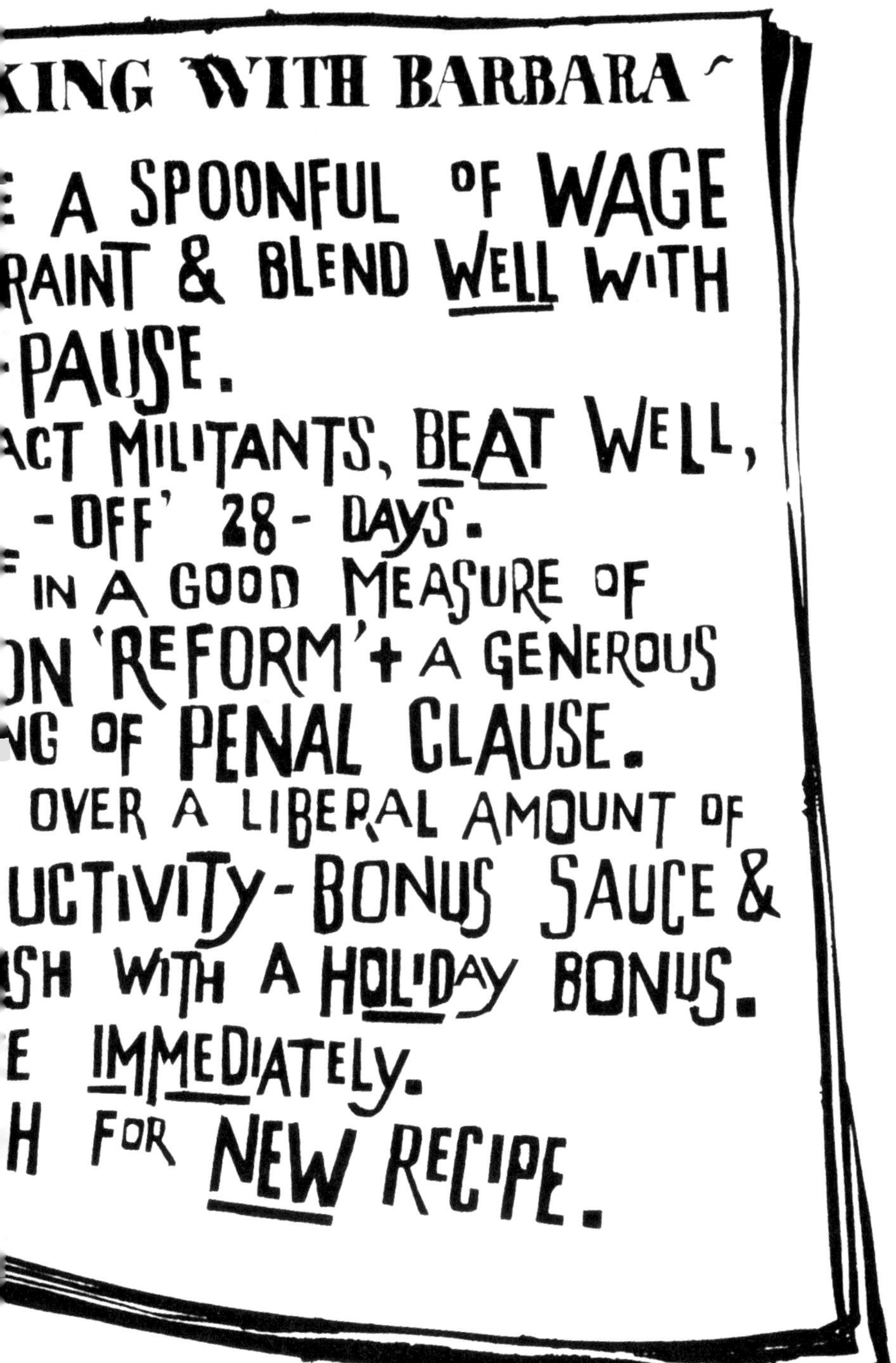

E A SPOONFUL OF WAGE
RAINT & BLEND WELL WITH
PAUSE.
ACT MILITANTS, BEAT WELL,
-OFF' 28-DAYS.
IN A GOOD MEASURE OF
ON 'REFORM'+ A GENEROUS
NG OF PENAL CLAUSE.
OVER A LIBERAL AMOUNT OF
UCTIVITY-BONUS SAUCE &
SH WITH A HOLIDAY BONUS.
E IMMEDIATELY.
H FOR NEW RECIPE.

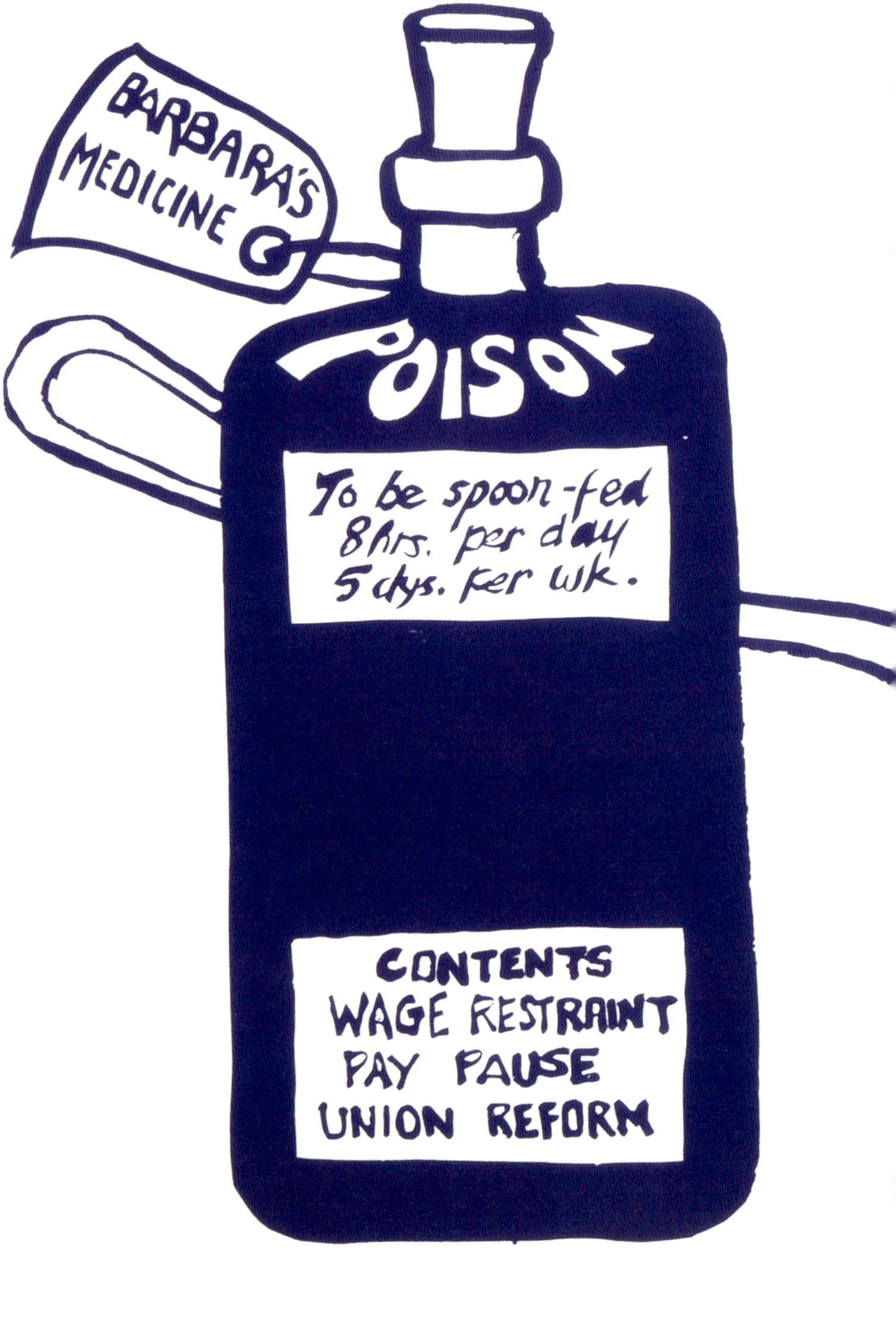

BARBARA'S MEDICINE
POISON
To be spoon-fed
8 hrs. per day
5 dys. per wk.
CONTENTS
WAGE RESTRAINT
PAY PAUSE
UNION REFORM

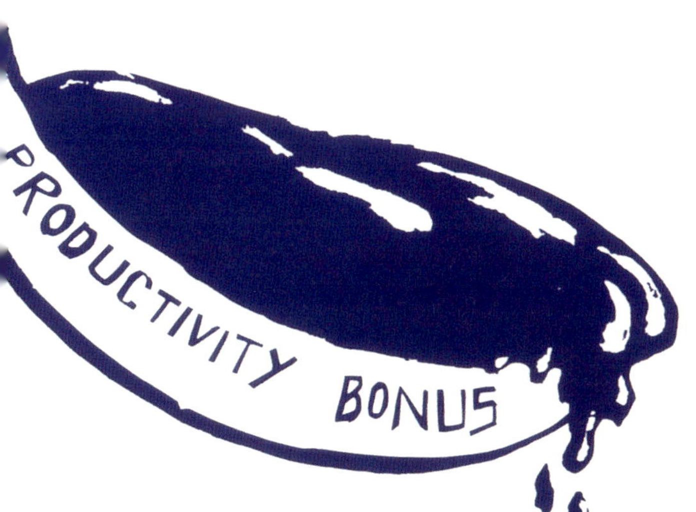

ARE **YOU** GOING TO

TAKE YOUR MEDICINE

AND.....

A SPOONFUL OF SUGAR?

FIGHT FACTORY CLOSURES-
NOT YOUR COLOURED WORKMATES

SAME BOSSES

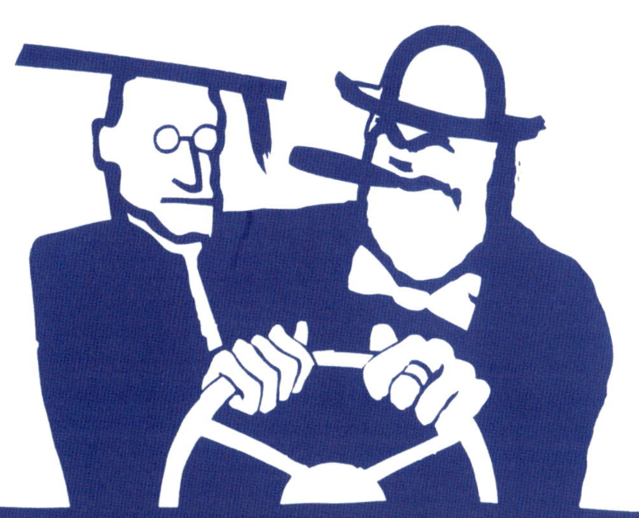

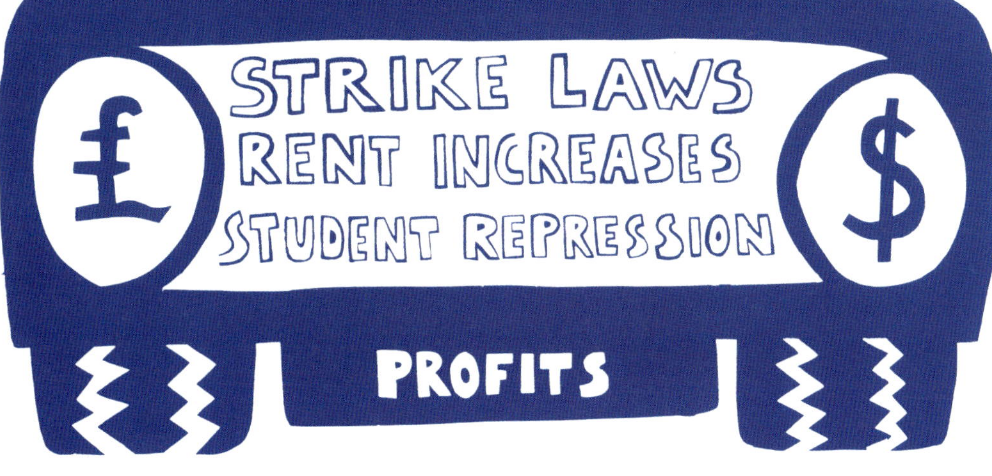

SAME FIGHT

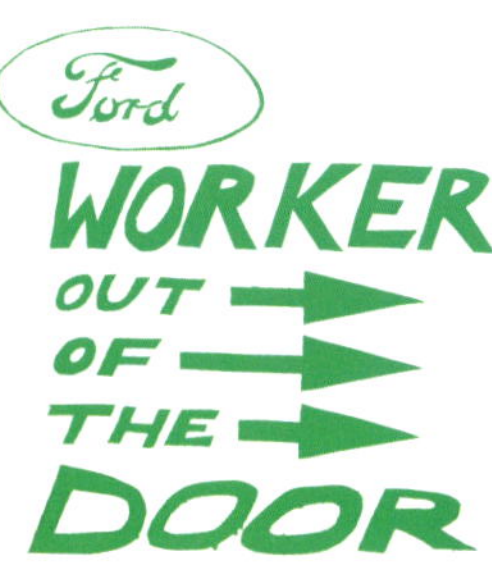

£20 BONUS
OUT OF THE
WINDOW
Ford
WORKER
OUT
OF
THE
DOOR

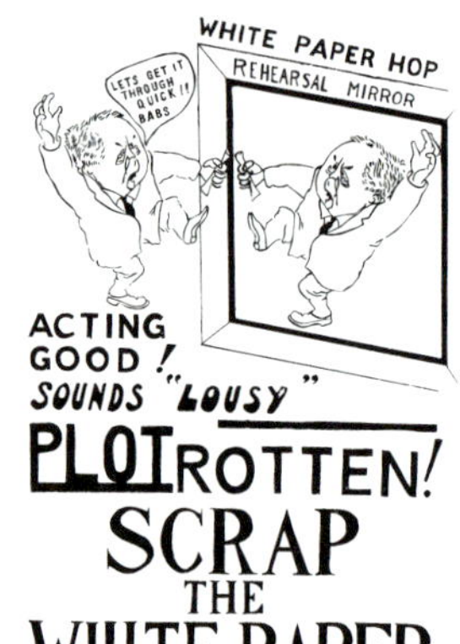

WHITE PAPER HOP
REHEARSAL MIRROR
LETS GET IT THROUGH QUICK IT BABS
ACTING
GOOD !
SOUNDS "LOUSY"
PLOT ROTTEN!
SCRAP
THE
WHITE PAPER

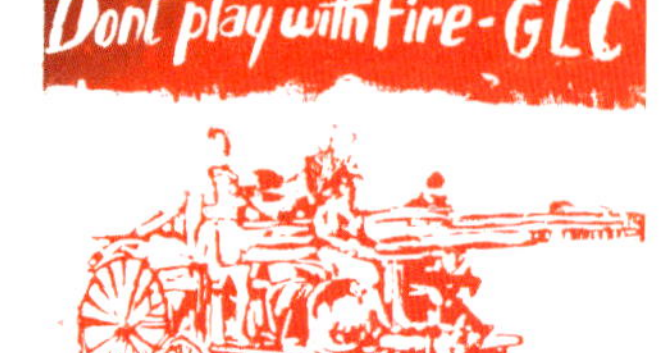

Don't play with Fire - GLC

GLC Bureaucracy
risks our lives
and Yours !

wandsworth young teacher
nut
MEETING with SPEAKERS
WORKING
CONDITIONS
IN SCHOOLS
Thursday 5 June
5.30
WANDSWORTH TOWN HALL

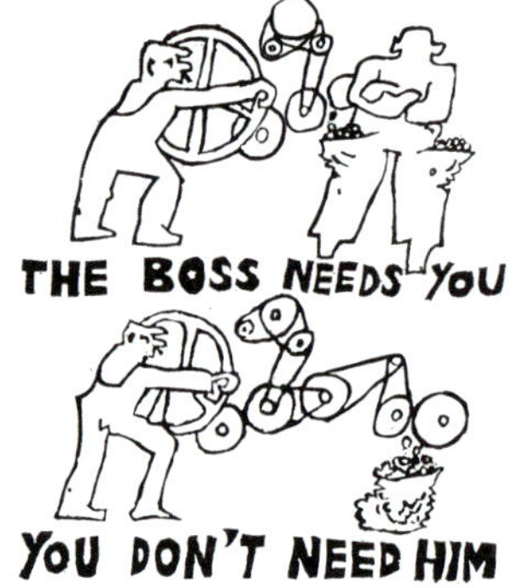

THE BOSS NEEDS YOU
YOU DON'T NEED HIM

PECKHAM PROJECT
BOVIS
"HEADS"
PRODUCED A BILL
FOR
CONSULTANTS FEE £20,000
PLUS
£900,000 FOR COMPLETION
BUT !!
CANNOT OR WILL NOT
PRODUCE A
PRODUCTIVITY   TARGET
BONUS SCHEME.
A
STOPPAGE COSTING £1,800, DAY

ROYAL
GROUP
DOCKS
CAMPAIGN
£6 FOR 8 HOURS
PIECEWORK
£30 FOR 40
HOUR WEEK
WE CAN WAIT
BUT IT MUST BE
6 FOR 8
NO TO PHASE 2
SHIFTWORK

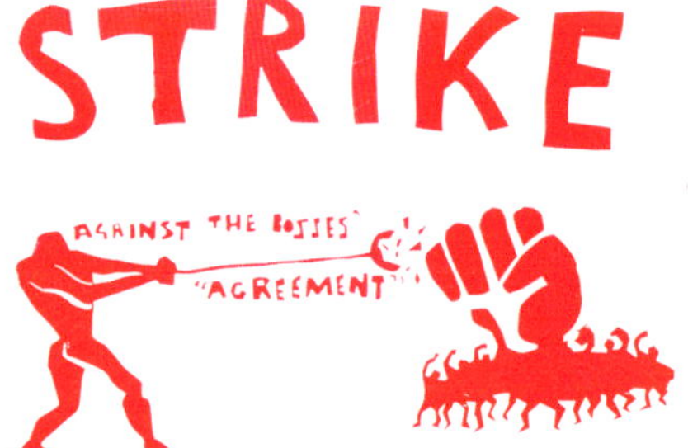

STRIKE
AGAINST THE BOSSES'
"AGREEMENT"

International Socialists
Public Meeting

FIGHT
UNEMPLOYMENT
SUPPORT
UPPER CLYDE
WORKERS

Co op Hall
129 Seven Sisters Rd Holloway N7

8.0pm
Monday 16th August
UCS Film/TU speakers

One day, three members of the Pan African Congress, wanting a poster, entered the Poster Workshop. Ten minutes later, the African National Congress arrived. An enormous row broke out. The ANC retreated. *Vuka*, which means 'wake up', was the PAC poster (p. 77) and *Wake Up!* was a handbill (p. 76). 'Izwe Lethu' means 'Our Land'. Sam later met an exiled leader of the PAC, who became upset when he discovered that lowlier members of the organisation had printed a poster without his permission. Why both organisations turned up at the Poster Workshop at the same time remains a mystery.

Robert Sobukwe (p. 79) left the ANC in 1959 to help found and become first President of the PAC. He led a demonstration against the hated Pass Laws on the same day as the Sharpeville massacre, was arrested and sent to Robben Island. Released in 1969, he was kept under house arrest until his death in 1978.

No Arms for South Africa (p. 80) protested against Ted Heath's Conservative Government lifting an arms embargo in 1970 which had been imposed by the previous Labour Government (though it had allowed the supply of spare parts). The Tories managed to sell some helicopters, but opposition in Britain and the Commonwealth prevented a major arms deal. The Anti-Apartheid movement had long campaigned against the supply of weapons and for an end to military collaboration. In the early 1960s, Britain had been South Africa's major arms supplier.

Sunny South Africa (p. 81) was the slogan of South African Airways. Like many posters printed at the Poster Workshop, it was a joint effort. It had been decided to use the slogan – but what image? Someone came up with the barbed wire, someone else drew it up. As soon as it had been printed, a team picked it up and it was fly-posted onto the front windows of South African Airways in Regent Street. The convoy of cars was spotted by a police surveillance team, who had a tip off about a possible bank raid. Fortunately the posters were already glued up when the cars were stopped at a red light in Bond Street. The fly-posting crew were fined next morning at Bow Street Magistrates Court.

The Nigerian civil war, 1967–70, was fought to prevent the secession of Biafra (p. 84). After independence in 1960, the resulting ill-conceived state, composed of various tribal, ethnic and religious groups led to conflict. And sadly still does today.

Anguilla, a very small Caribbean island, had been a British colony. In 1967 Britain proposed uniting it with the marginally larger island of St Kitts when they both gained internal autonomy. The Anguillans were outraged and declared independence. The British over-reacted and sent in a crack battalion of 300 men. They were met by flag waving local citizens demanding to be returned to British rule. The event was dubbed 'Britain's Bay of Piglets' (p. 78).

Régis Debray (p. 84) was a French journalist who was arrested and imprisoned in Bolivia in April 1967 where he had gone to interview Che Guevara. Guevara was captured and executed by the military the following October. Debray was sentenced to between 17 and 30 years in prison. After an international outcry, he was released in 1970.

Huey Newton (p. 84) co-founded the Black Panther Party in the USA with Bobby Seale in 1966. Armed Black Panthers aimed to protect ethnic minorities against police violence and involved themselves in community work, including providing free breakfasts for poor children. He was sentenced to between 2 and 15 years for voluntary manslaughter of a police officer. Public pressure helped free him in 1970. He was shot dead in Oakland, California in 1989.

The Poster Workshop was asked to print *Boycott* and *Don't Shop* (p. 79) in support of a strike by the United Farm Workers Union against Californian grape growers who refused to recognise trade union representation. Most of the workers were low-paid immigrants. The strike began in 1965 and lasted more than five years. Due mainly to a large consumer boycott, the union eventually succeeded in reaching a free collective bargaining agreement with the grape growers.

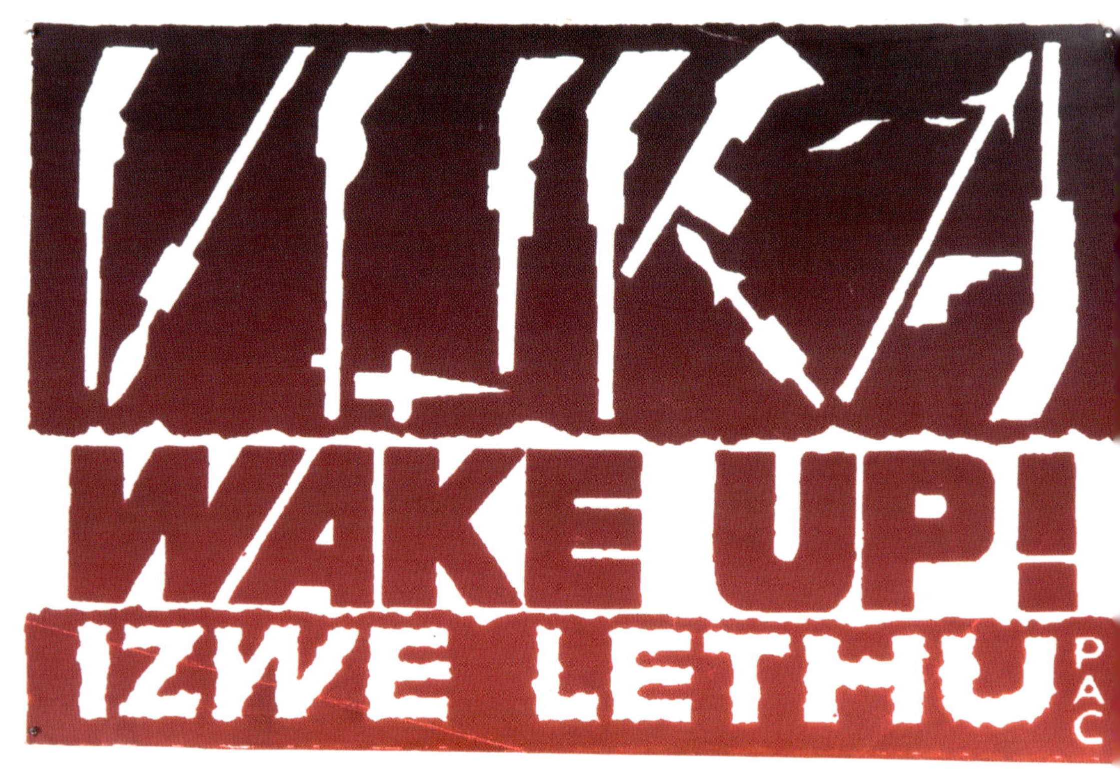

VUKA
WAKE UP!
IZWE LETHU
PAC

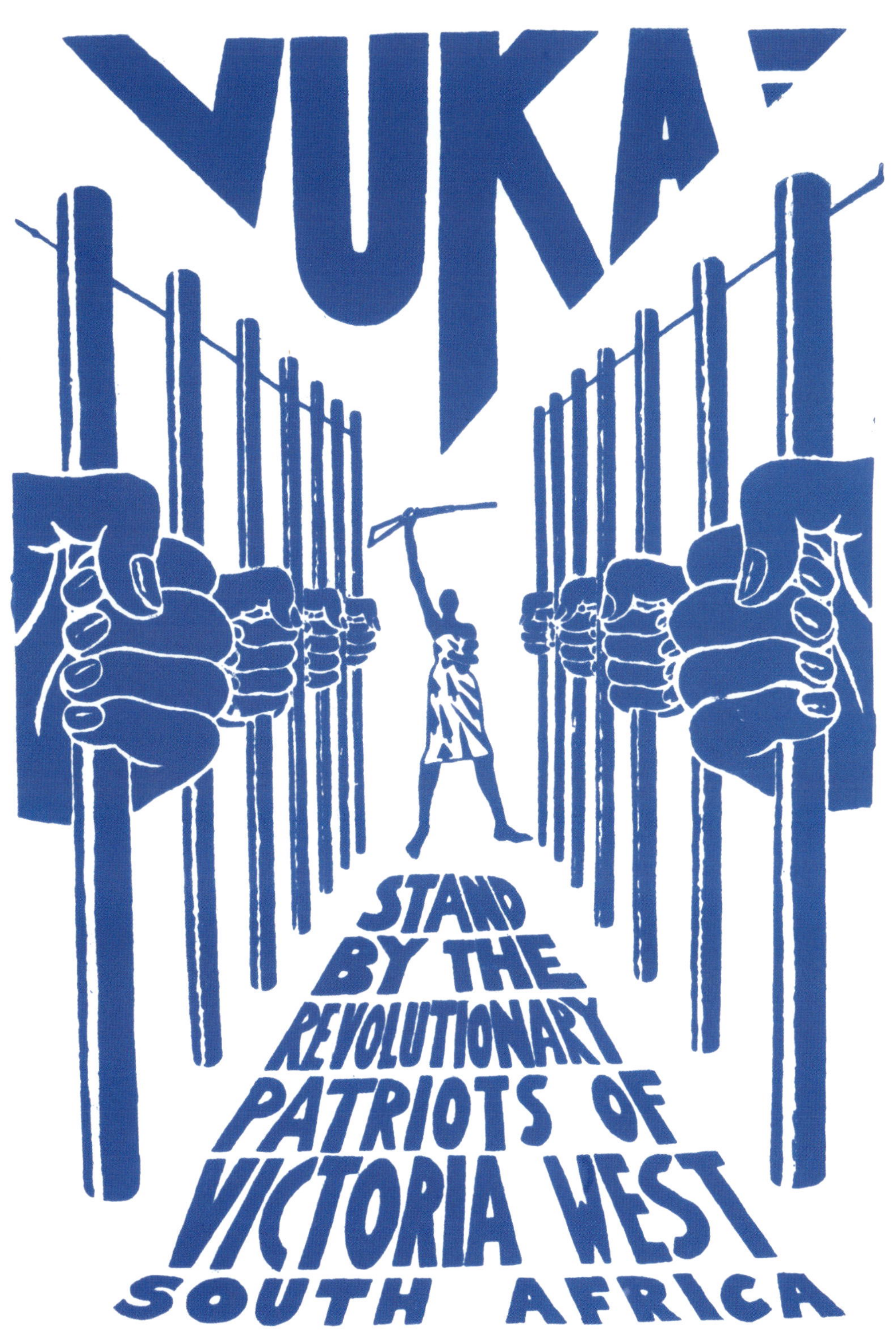

VUKA!
STAND
BY THE
REVOLUTIONARY
PATRIOTS OF
VICTORIA WEST
SOUTH AFRICA

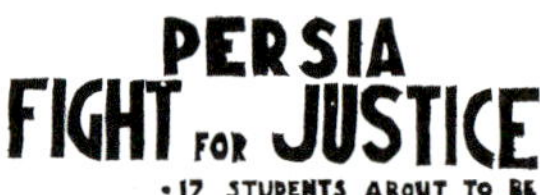
PERSIA
FIGHT FOR JUSTICE
17 STUDENTS ABOUT TO BE TRIED IN SECRET MILITARY COURT.
8 ABOUT TO BE SHOT.
ACT NOW
DEMAND A PUBLIC TRIAL WITH FOREIGN OBSERVERS
THE SHAH OF PERSIA'S REGIME HAS PRESS-GANGED HUNDREDS INTO MILITARY SERVICE.
NO POLICE AND MILITARY INTERVENTION IN UNIVERSITIES
MARCH WITH US!
TO THE IRANIAN EMBASSY
SAT. 30TH NOV. AT 2.30 STRATFORD PL. (BOND ST.)
IRAN DEFENSE COM. C/O POSTER WORK. 61 CAMDEN RD.

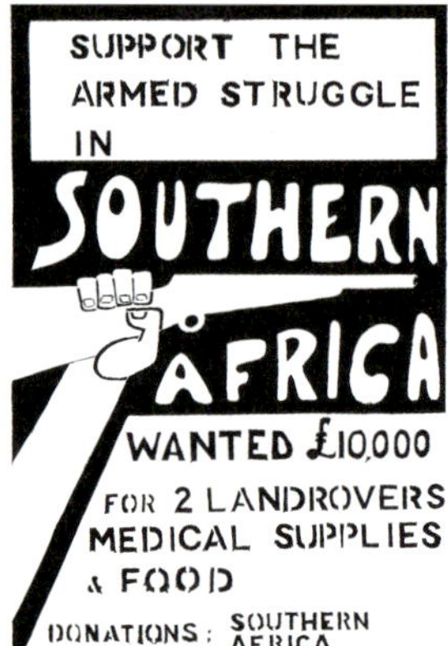
SUPPORT THE ARMED STRUGGLE IN
SOUTHERN AFRICA
WANTED £10,000
FOR 2 LANDROVERS MEDICAL SUPPLIES & FOOD
DONATIONS: SOUTHERN AFRICA APPEAL
103 Borough High St   SE 1

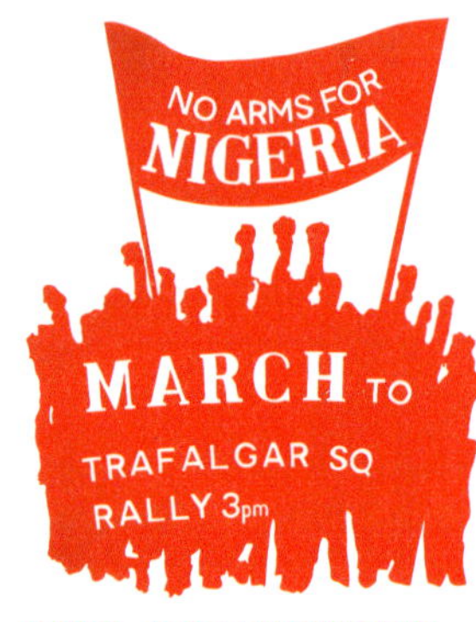
NO ARMS FOR NIGERIA
MARCH TO TRAFALGAR SQ RALLY 3pm
MEET – PARLIAMENT HILL
SUN. 26 OCT. 1.30pm

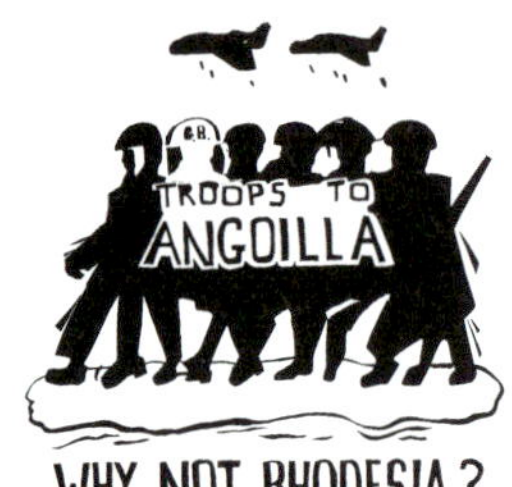
TROOPS TO ANGOILLA
WHY NOT RHODESIA?
ALL BLACK AND PROGRESSIVE PEOPLE DEMONSTRATE AGAINST BRITISH IMPERIALIST INTERVENTION IN ANGUILLA : SPEAKERS CORNER · HYDE PARK
PANTHERS UK PA
SUN. MAR. 23. 3pm

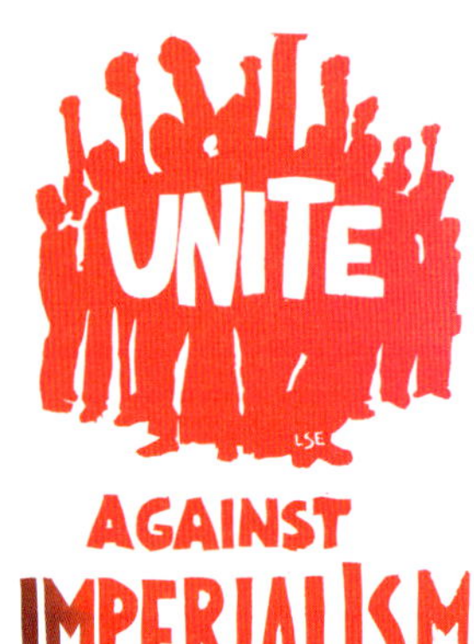
UNITE
LSE
AGAINST IMPERIALISM

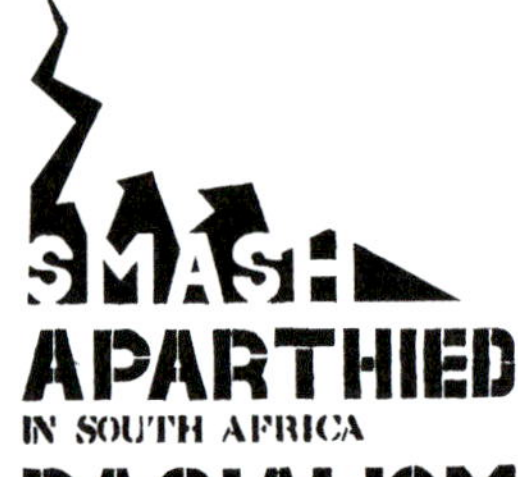
SMASH APARTHIED
IN SOUTH AFRICA
RACIALISM
IN LEICESTER
DEMONSTRATION THURSDAY 15 MAY
SPINNEY HILL PARK
7.0 PM

FISH & CHIPS
on the COSTA BRAVA
BUT TORTURE IN MADRID

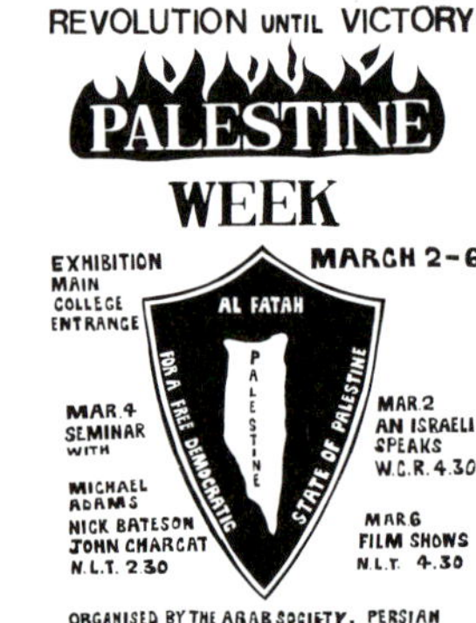
REVOLUTION UNTIL VICTORY
PALESTINE WEEK
EXHIBITION MAIN COLLEGE ENTRANCE
MARCH 2-6
AL FATAH
FOR A FREE DEMOCRATIC STATE OF PALESTINE
PALESTINE
MAR. 4 SEMINAR WITH
MICHAEL ADAMS NICK BATESON JOHN CHARCAT N.L.T. 2.30
MAR. 2 AN ISRAELI SPEAKS W.C.R. 4.30
MAR 6 FILM SHOWS N.L.T. 4.30
ORGANISED BY THE ARAB SOCIETY, PERSIAN AND SOCIALIST SOCIETIES
QUEEN MARY COLLEGE. MILE END RD. E.1.

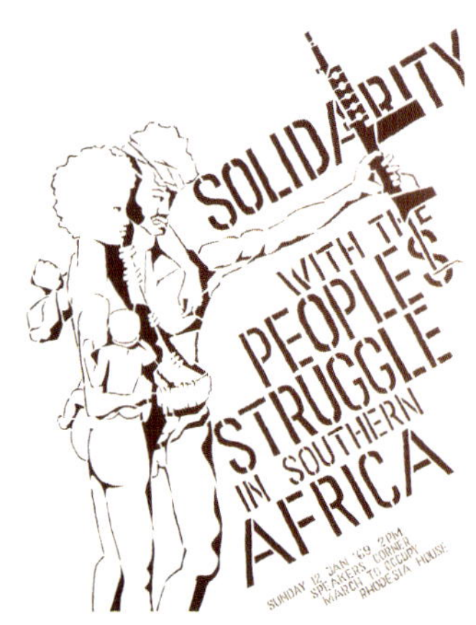
SOLIDARITY
WITH THE PEOPLES STRUGGLE IN SOUTHERN AFRICA
SUNDAY 12 JAN '69. 2 PM
SPEAKERS CORNER
MARCH TO BEGIN
RHODESIA HOUSE

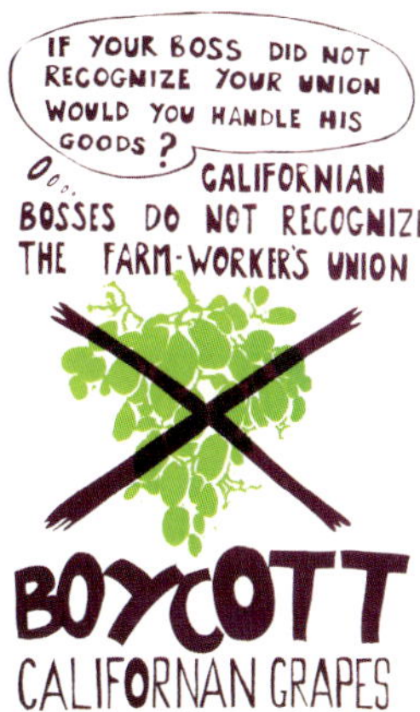

FREE
SOBUKWE

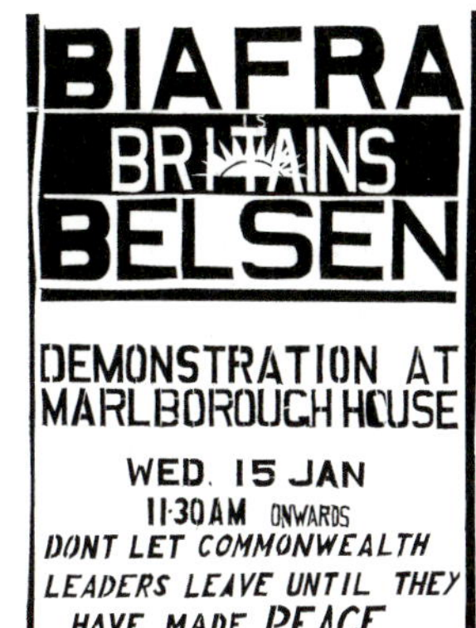

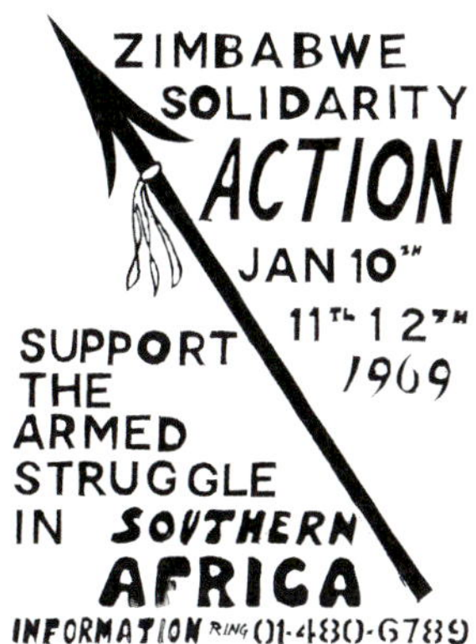

DON'T SHOP SAFEWAYS — SUPPORT U.S. FARMWORKERS

FORWARD TO AZANIAN SOCIALIST REVOLUTION

saturday 22nd march

10 TH YEAR OF PAN AFRICANIST CONGRESS
9 TH ANNIVERSARY OF SHARPEVILLE BARBARISM
6 TH YEAR OF SOBUKWE'S INCARCERATION ON MAKANA ISLAND

pac speakers
film:the mad masters
(first and only public showing)

7.30–11.0pm
all saints hall
powis gardens – off
westbourne pk rd
w11

donations

Public Business UGM
FRIDAY 29   1pm
union Small Lounge
MOTION

South Afvican
Students Jailed
Your Goverment
Supports this
NAZI Regime

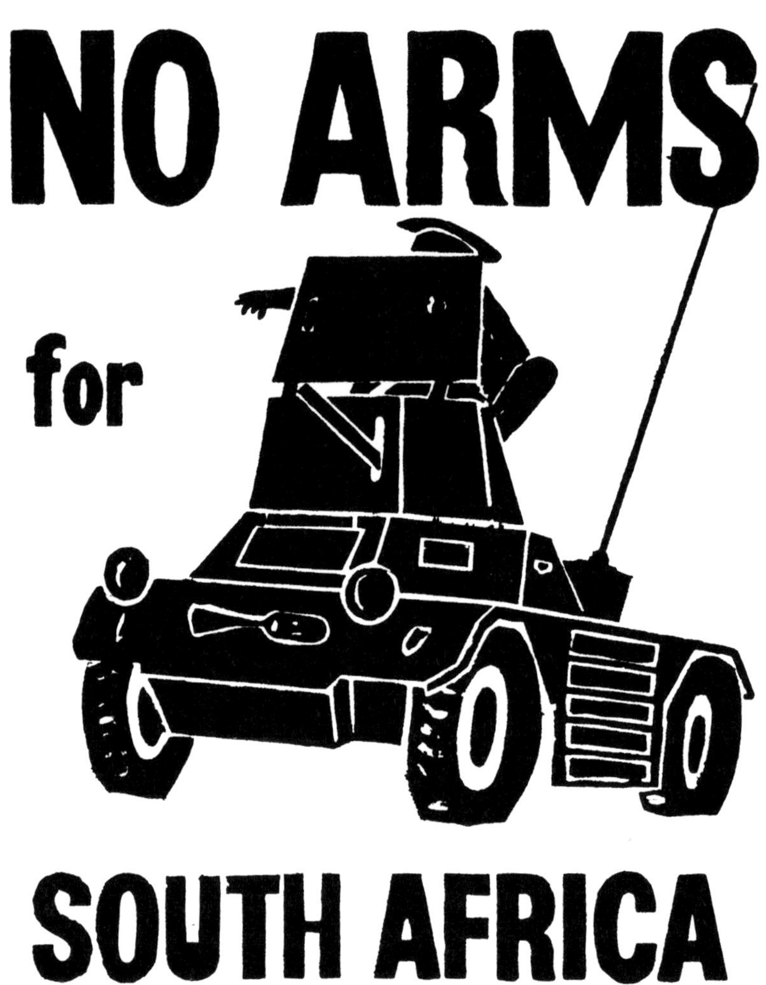
NO ARMS
for
SOUTH AFRICA

SUNNY
SOUTH AFRICA

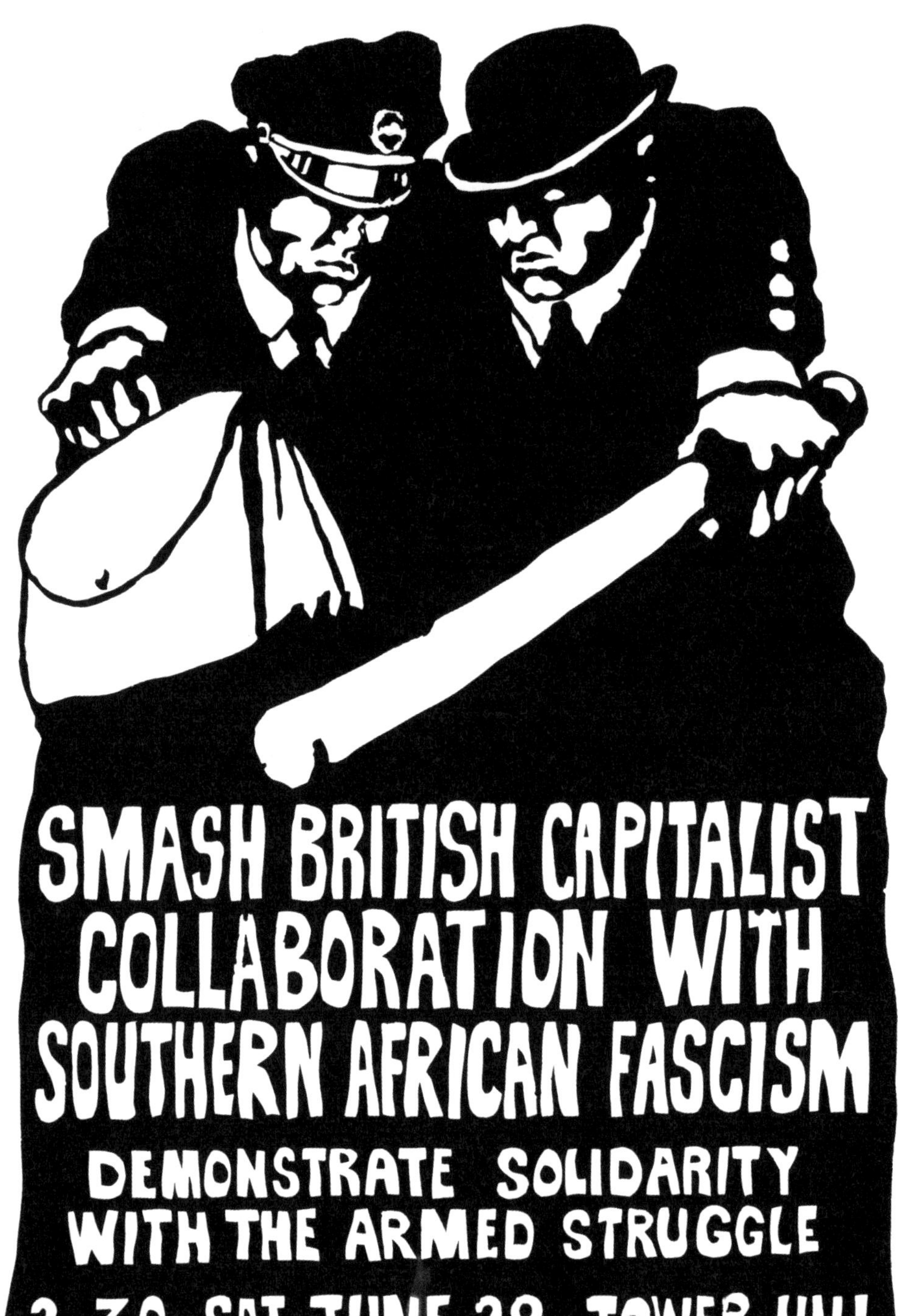

SMASH BRITISH CAPITALIST
COLLABORATION WITH
SOUTHERN AFRICAN FASCISM
DEMONSTRATE SOLIDARITY
WITH THE ARMED STRUGGLE
2-30 SAT JUNE 28 TOWER HILL

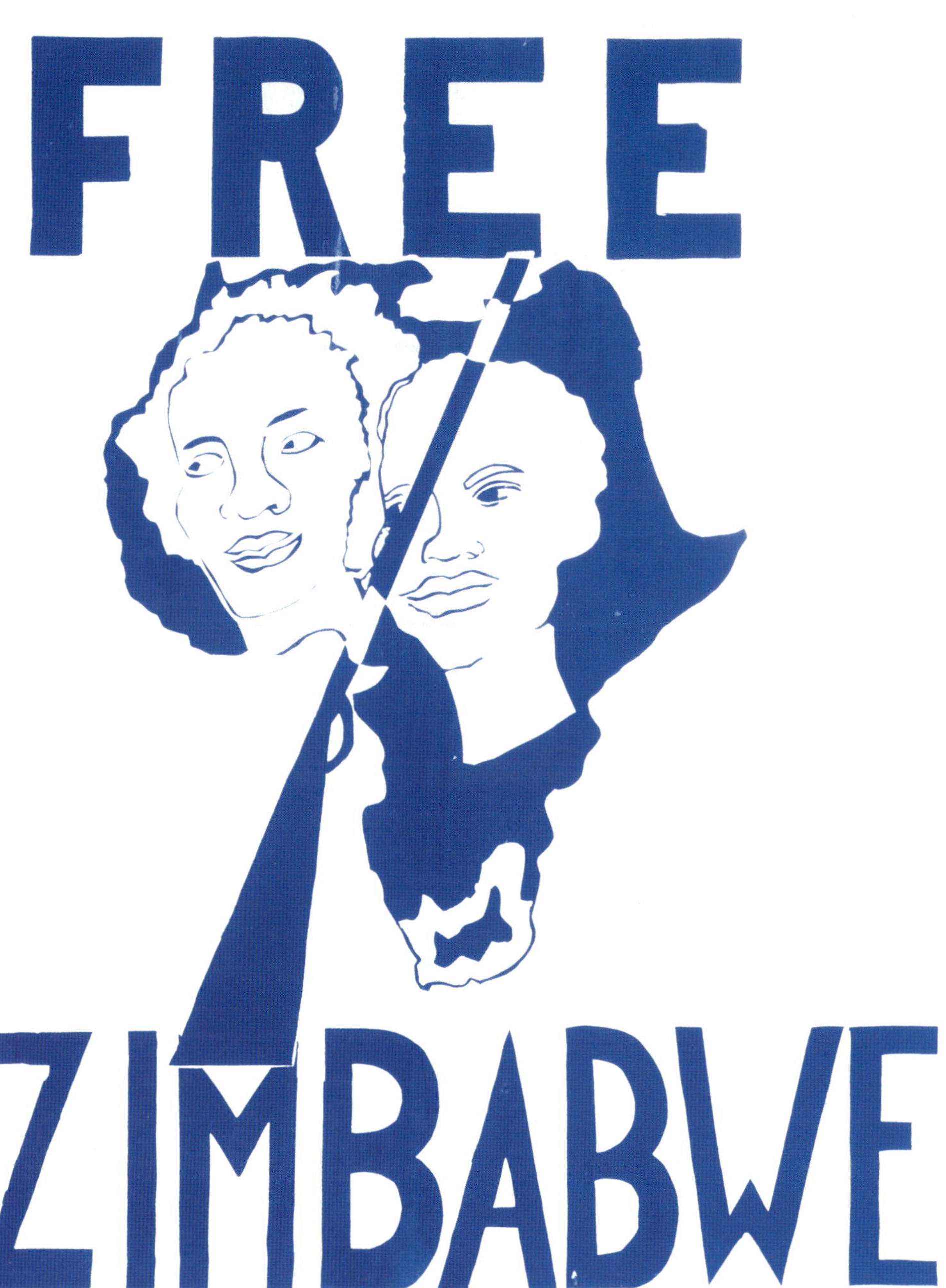
FREE
ZIMBABWE

CUBA TEACH IN AND RAVE 5/-
THE ROUND HOUSE CHALK FARM ROAD NW1

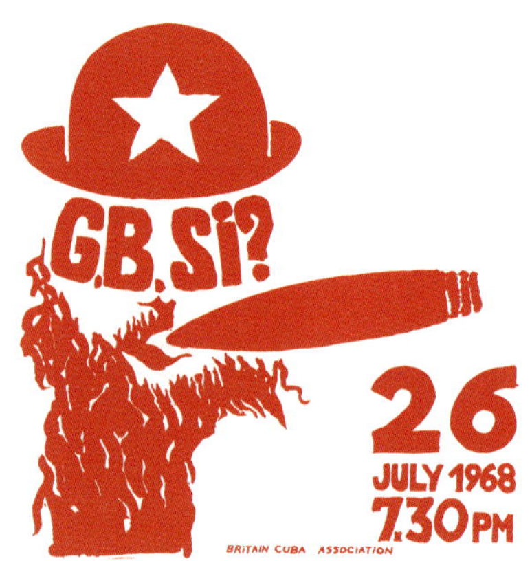

G.B. Si?
26
JULY 1968
7.30 PM
BRITAIN CUBA ASSOCIATION

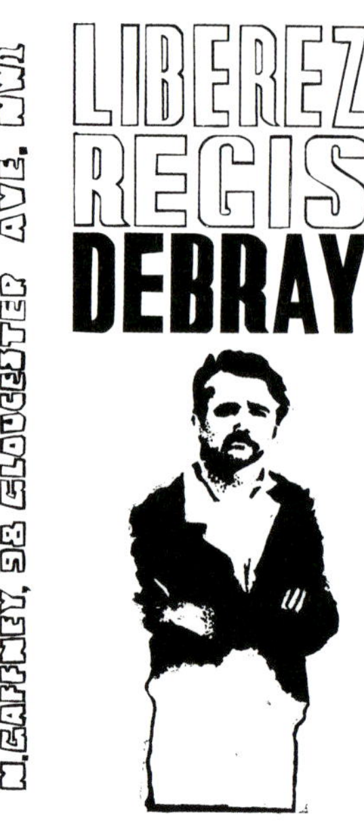

LIBEREZ REGIS DEBRAY
N. GAFFNEY, 58 GLOUCESTER AVE. NW1

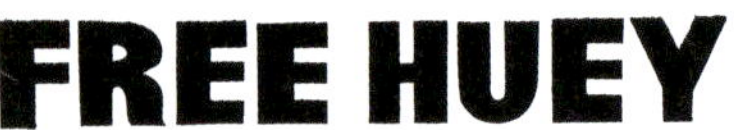
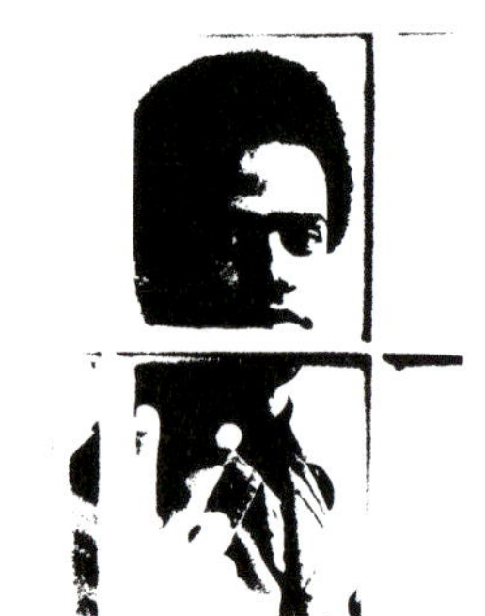

FREE HUEY
THE SPIRIT OF THE PEOPLE
IS GREATER THAN
THE MAN'S TECHNOLOGY

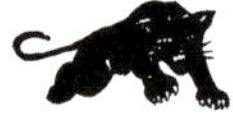

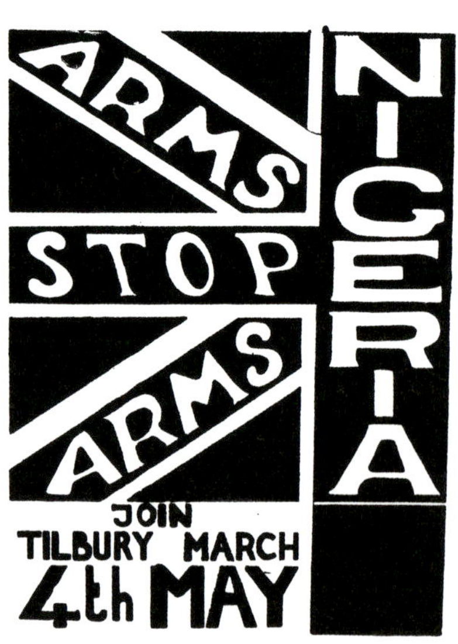

ARMS STOP ARMS NIGERIA
JOIN
TILBURY MARCH
4th MAY

WE ARE ALL
Foreign
SCUM

Unity Theatre (p. 88) was founded in 1936 by the Rebel Players, after years of performing on street corners. In 1937, it moved to a former chapel in Goldington Street, Camden Town. By the mid 1940s there were 250 branches throughout Britain, although Liverpool Unity Theatre is the sole survivor still operating. It was closely allied to the Communist Party and grew out of the Workers Theatre Movement in the East End. It used agit-prop techniques whose off the cuff style often fell foul of the Lord Chamberlain's theatre censorship, which itself was finally abolished in 1968. Unity provided a wide range of activities including political lectures, film shows, dances and music. It staged the first Brecht play in Britain and was a training ground for many in theatre, such as Lionel Bart, Michael Gambon, and Bob Hoskins. A notable production was *Harold Muggins is a Martyr*, a collaboration between John Arden, Margaret d'Arcy and the Poster Workshop benefactors, the Cartoon Archetypal Slogan Theatre. The play parodied Harold Wilson's Britain. Muggins was a rundown café owner forced to pay protection money to gangsters (aka the USA).

Soon after the Poster Workshop opened, the Roundhouse in Chalk Farm offered them the job of designing and making the giant billboards advertising their productions. Billie Old and Sam began work, but it soon became obvious that this was a full time job, so the Poster Workshop handed over to Billie who remained as the sign-writer at the Roundhouse until 1974.

The founder of Black Arts (p. 87), Michael de Freitas, was a one time Rachman enforcer and pimp who remade himself as a black revolutionary under the name Michael X. He helped start the drugs charity Release, the London Free School and the Notting Hill Carnival with John 'Hoppy' Hopkins in 1967. Money went missing and, after assaulting a man at the commune he had founded, Black House, he fled to Trinidad where he was executed after committing murder.

POSTER
WORKSHOP
BENEFIT

c.a.s.t. - muggins awakening
& other plays
angry arts film society
- the columbia revolt
agit - prop street players

JAN 10 - 7.30

all saints hall
powis gardens
w.11   admission 5s

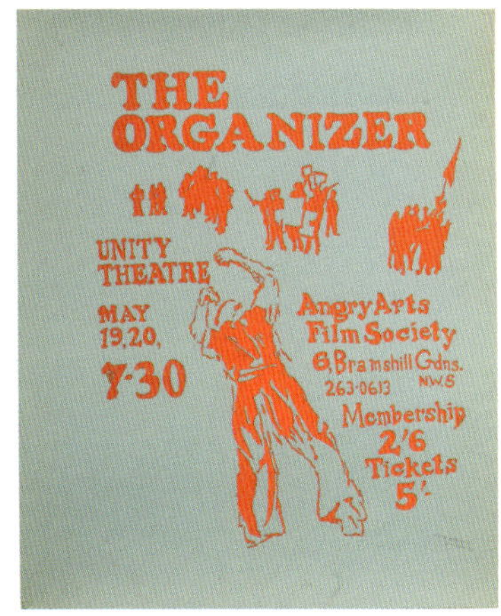

THE
ORGANIZER
UNITY
THEATRE
MAY
19,20,
7·30
Angry Arts
Film Society
6, Bramshill Gdns.
263·0613 NW.5
Membership
2/6
Tickets
5/-

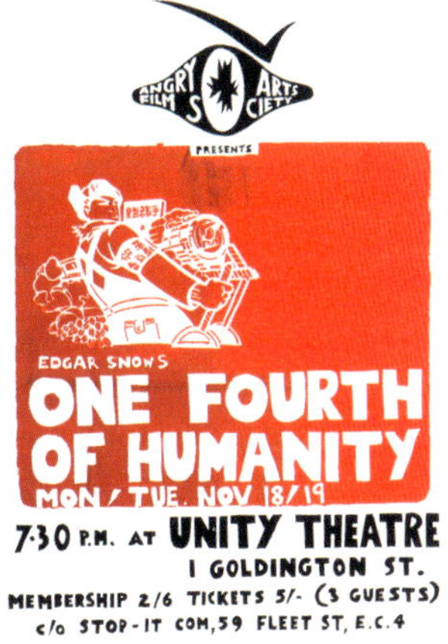

ANGRY ARTS FILM SOCIETY
PRESENTS
EDGAR SNOWS
ONE FOURTH
OF HUMANITY
MON / TUE. NOV 18/19
7·30 P.M. AT UNITY THEATRE
1 GOLDINGTON ST.
MEMBERSHIP 2/6 TICKETS 5/- (3 GUESTS)
C/O STOP-IT COM, 59 FLEET ST, E.C.4

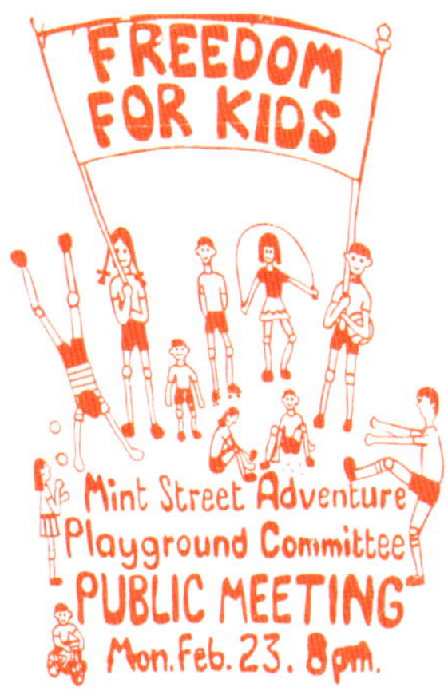

FREEDOM
FOR KIDS
Mint Street Adventure
Playground Committee
PUBLIC MEETING
Mon. Feb. 23. 8pm.

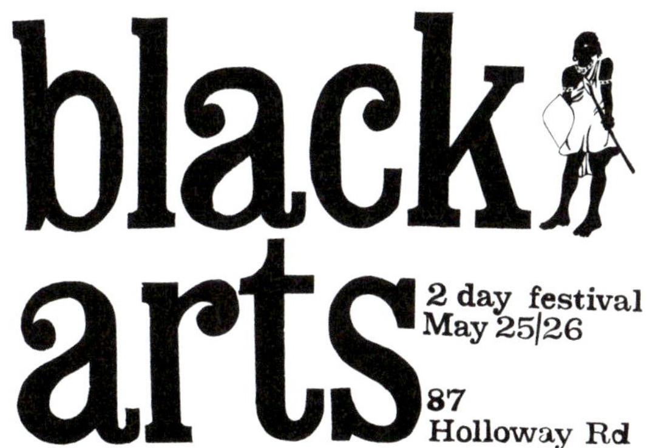

black
arts
2 day festival
May 25/26
87
Holloway Rd

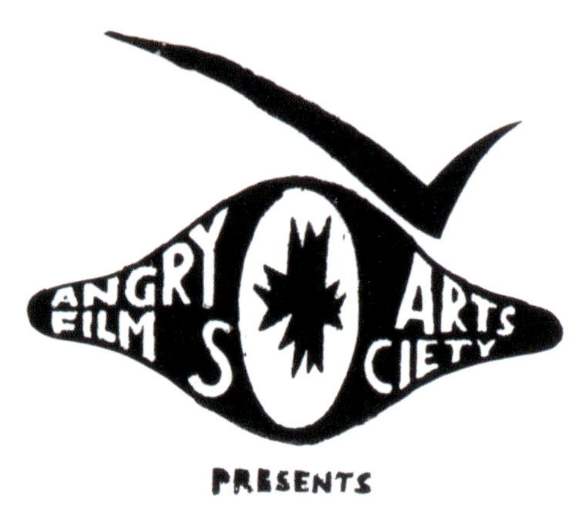

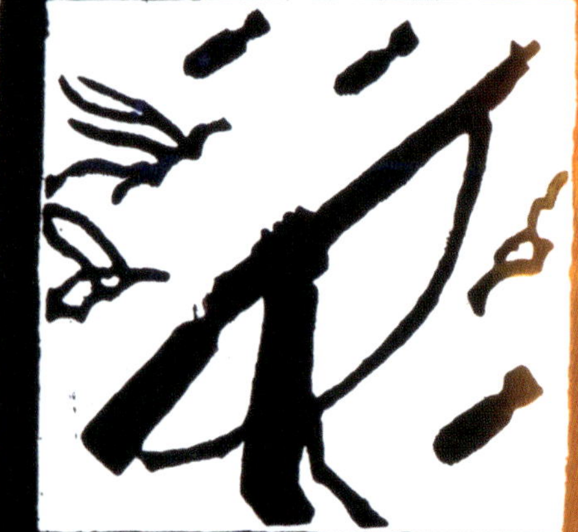

7.30 P.M. AT **UNITY THEATRE**
1 GOLDINGTON ST.
MEMBERSHIP 2/6 TICKETS 5/- (3 GUESTS)
c/o STOP-IT COM, 59 FLEET ST, E.C.4

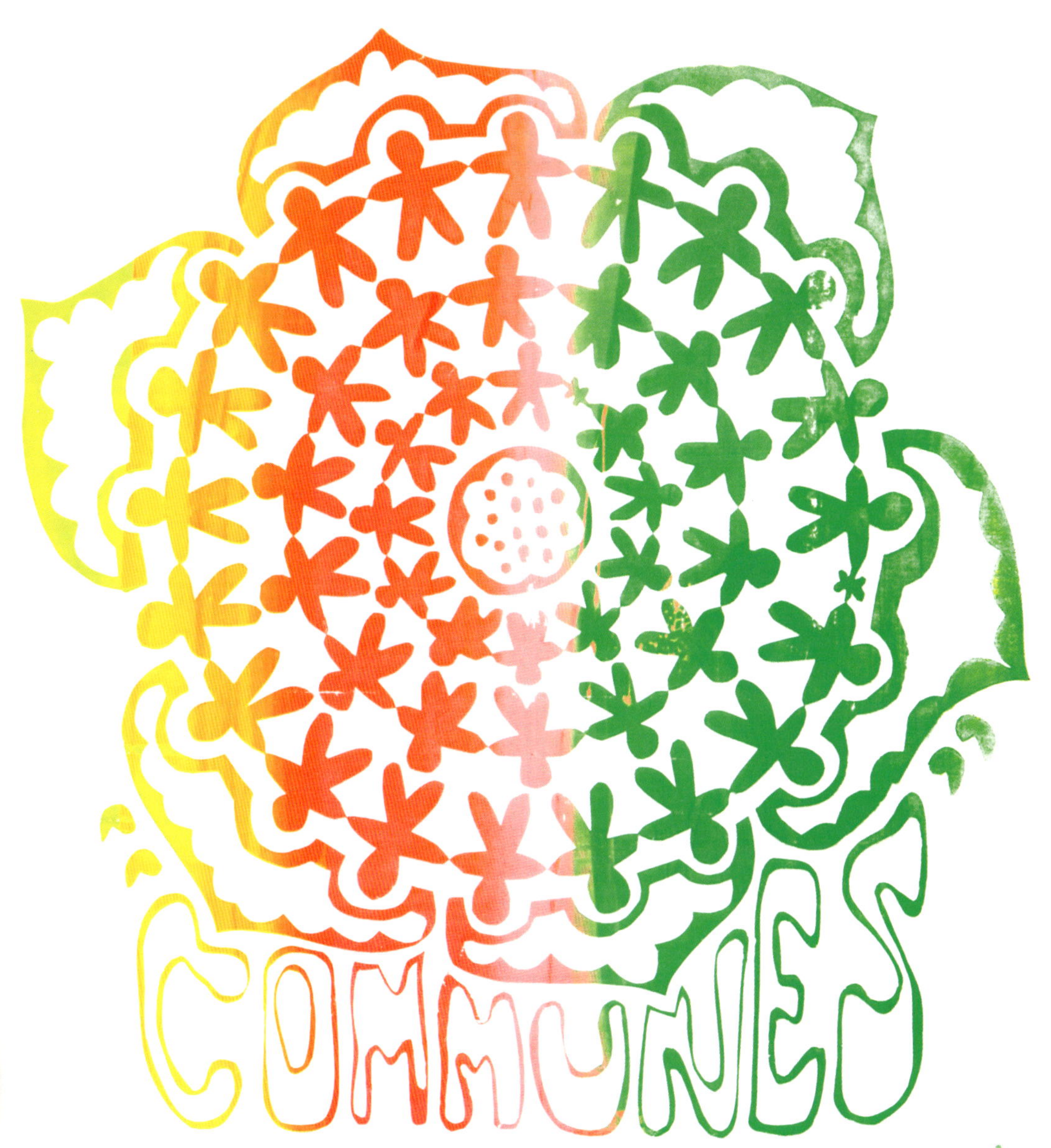

COMMUNES
journal of the commune movement
'bit', 141 westbourne park road,
london w.11.   01-229-8219

BAZAAR

SATURDAY NOV 30TH 2PM
CONGREGATIONAL HALL
LYNDHURST ROAD ROSSLYN HILL

HOME-MADE-CAKES
POTTERY·CHRISTMAS·CARDS
GOOD-AS-NEW-CLOTHES
★ BOOKS · TOYS ★
HOUSEHOLD GOODS
BOOKS ····· GIFTS
MADAME-ZAZA·FORTUNE TELLER
☮ REFRESHMENTS

ENTRANCE 6' CND ☮

POPLAR LIMEHOUSE TENANTS ASSOC.
SPONSOR A

GRAND **DANCE**

EAST INDIA HALL
EAST INDIA DOCK RD, E.14.
SAT 29TH MAR
1969
TOP LINE MUSIC
7 30 PM   11 30 PM
ADMISSION 7/6 TICKETS ONLY
LICENSED BAR - FREE BUFFET

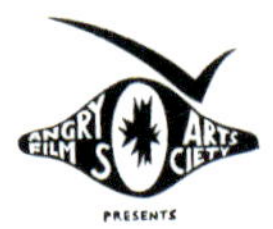

THE 17TH PARALLEL
JORIS IVENS

MON/TUES
JAN 13/14

7·30 P.M. AT **UNITY THEATRE**
1 GOLDINGTON ST.
MEMBERSHIP 2/6 TICKETS 5/- (3 GUESTS)
c/o STOP-IT COM, 59 FLEET ST, E.C.4

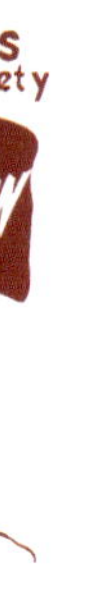

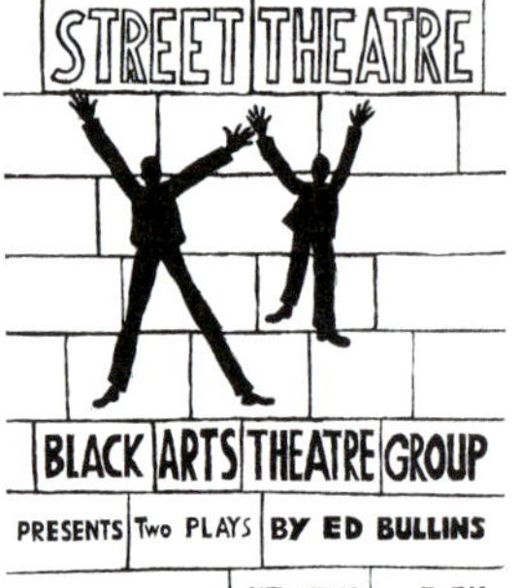

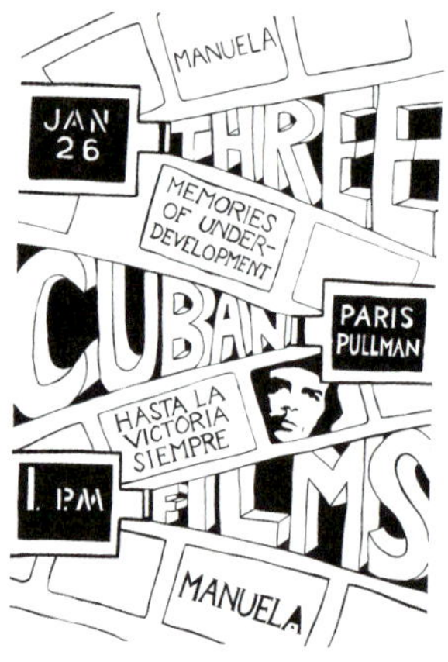

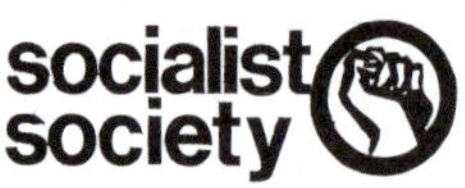

date
time
place

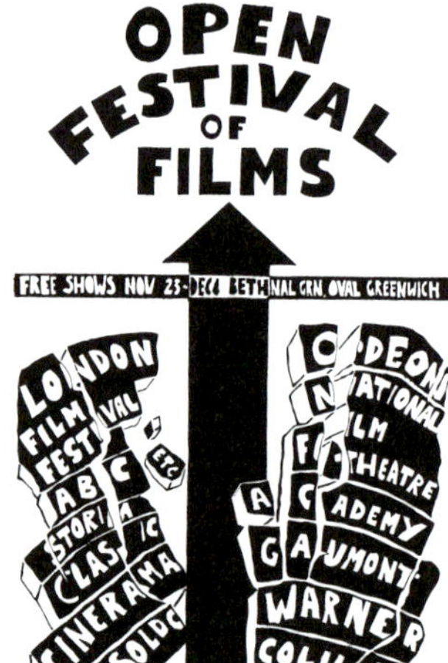

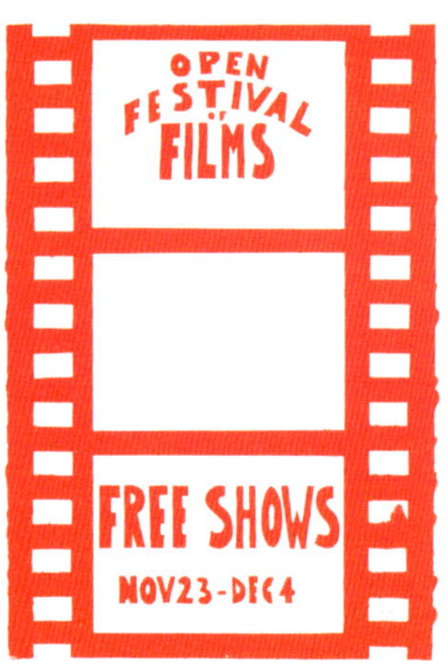

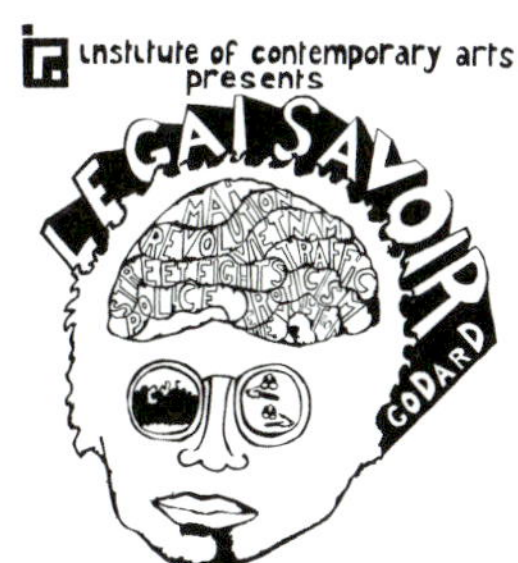
institute of contemporary arts
presents
LE GAI SAVOIR
GODARD
ICA, NASH HOUSE, THE MALL
from July the 12th, a month season
Sat. Sun. Mon. at 6 and 8 pm
Box office 930.6393

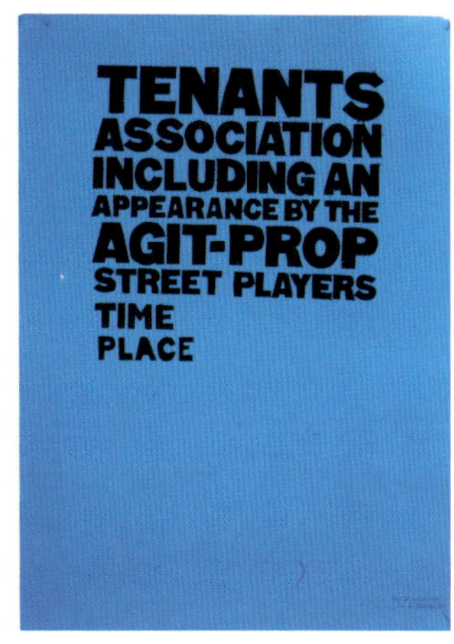
McCARTHY
BENEFIT DANCE
FRI 23 JUL
8 PM-12 AM
30 P
LATE BAR
MUSIC: THIRD WORLD WAR
ROXANA
QUARK
& others
STUDENTS UNION
CITY UNIVERSITY
NORTHAMPTON SQ. EC1
Angel tube

TENANTS
ASSOCIATION
INCLUDING AN
APPEARANCE BY THE
AGIT-PROP
STREET PLAYERS
TIME
PLACE

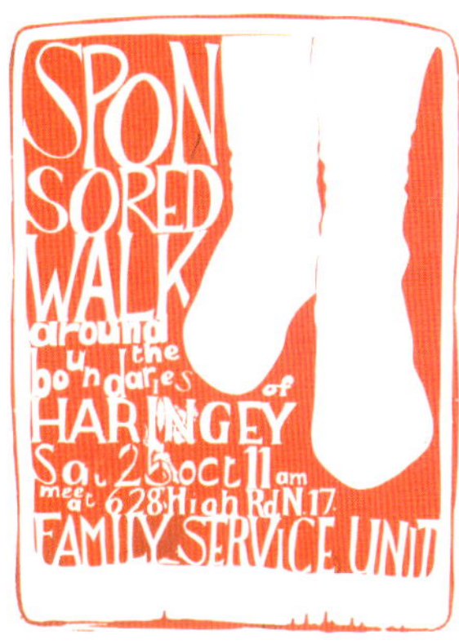
SPONSORED WALK
around the boundaries of HARINGEY
Sat. 25 Oct 11 am
meet at 628 High Rd N17.
FAMILY SERVICE UNIT

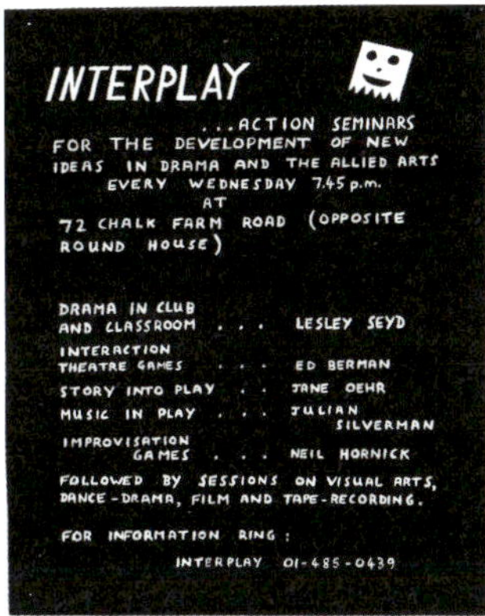
INTERPLAY
...ACTION SEMINARS
FOR THE DEVELOPMENT OF NEW
IDEAS IN DRAMA AND THE ALLIED ARTS
EVERY WEDNESDAY 7.45 p.m.
AT
72 CHALK FARM ROAD (OPPOSITE
ROUND HOUSE)
DRAMA IN CLUB
AND CLASSROOM ... LESLEY SEYD
INTERACTION
THEATRE GAMES ... ED BERMAN
STORY INTO PLAY ... JANE OEHR
MUSIC IN PLAY ... JULIAN SILVERMAN
IMPROVISATION
GAMES ... NEIL HORNICK
FOLLOWED BY SESSIONS ON VISUAL ARTS,
DANCE-DRAMA, FILM AND TAPE-RECORDING.
FOR INFORMATION RING:
INTERPLAY 01-485-0439

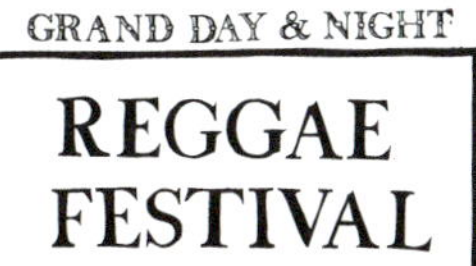
GRAND DAY & NIGHT
REGGAE FESTIVAL
2 PM - MIDNIGHT APRIL 7"
AT CATFORD COOP HALL
22 BROWNHILL RD S.E.6.
with
STEVE
AND THE SUCESSION
&
COUNT NEVILLE
MUSICAL ENCHANTER
BE SURE TO GO

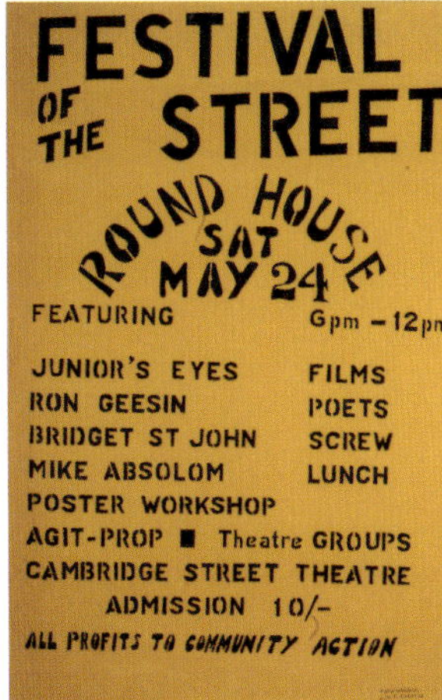
FESTIVAL OF THE STREET
ROUND HOUSE
SAT MAY 24
FEATURING
6 pm - 12 pm
JUNIOR'S EYES   FILMS
RON GEESIN   POETS
BRIDGET ST JOHN   SCREW
MIKE ABSOLOM   LUNCH
POSTER WORKSHOP
AGIT-PROP ■ Theatre GROUPS
CAMBRIDGE STREET THEATRE
ADMISSION 10/-
ALL PROFITS TO COMMUNITY ACTION

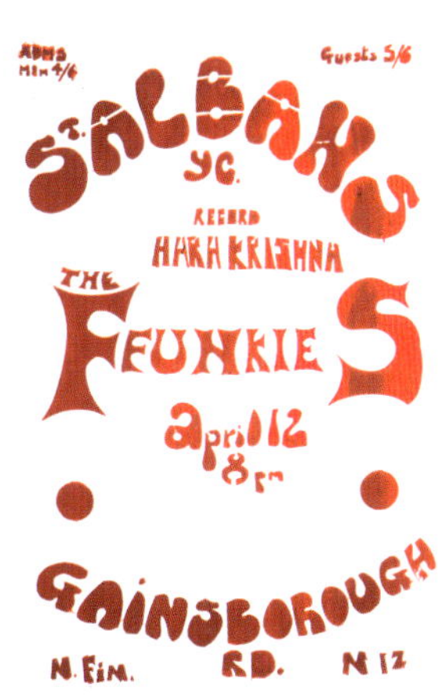
ADMS MEM 4/6   Guests 5/6
St. ALBANS Y.C.
RECORD
HARE KRISHNA
THE FFUNKIES
April 12
8 pm
GAINSBOROUGH
N. FIN.   RD.   N 12

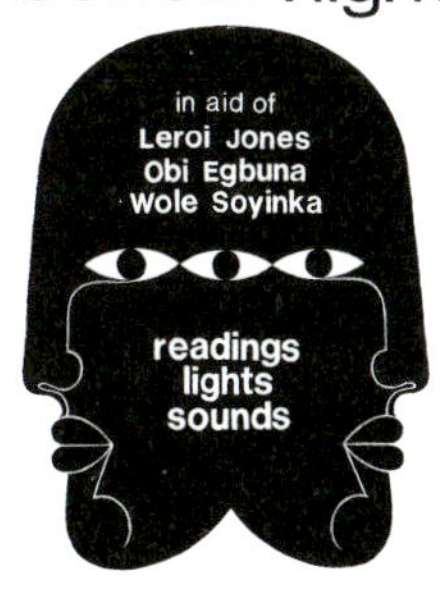
THIRD WORLD
benefit night
in aid of
Leroi Jones
Obi Egbuna
Wole Soyinka
readings
lights
sounds
SUN. AUG. 25th 7.30 pm   ROUND HOUSE
5/. ENTRANCE   CONTRIBUTIONS

Housing and Squatting

Housing, then as now, was a big issue, but people then were more likely to take the law into their own hands. The London Squatters Campaign was set up in November 1968 to occupy unused and empty property and rehouse homeless families living in inhuman conditions, to encourage further direct action, and to radicalise the struggle for decent housing for all. Squatting was both 'a symbolic direct action and a do-it-yourself solution to homelessness'.

Squatting required publicity both to put pressure on local authorities and to minimise the risk of eviction or arrest. The LSC was always very careful to pay the rates to the local council as well as the electricity, gas and water bills to avoid accusations of theft. Squatting in residential property became a crime in 2012, and can now carry a 6 month prison sentence, a £5000 fine or both.

OCCUPY
EMPTY
PROPERTY
LANDLORDS OUT !

HARLOW TENANTS ACTION COMMITTEE

HOMES
FOR
PEOPLE
NOT FOR
PROFIT

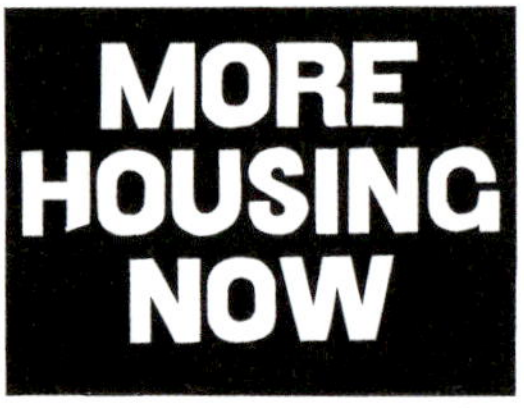

HACKNEY CONSERVATIVE COUNCIL HAVE CUT BUILDING BY 60%

MORE
HOUSING
NOW

NORTH LONDON
SQUATTERS

↑MARCH↑
→TO THE TOWN HALL←
↓DEMONSTRATE↓
→AGAINST REDBRIDGE COUNCIL→
↓OCCUPY AND RESTORE↓
A HOME FOR A HOMELESS FAMILY
→BRING YOUR OWN TOOLS←

SUPPORT THE SQUATTERS

JULY 15 · 6ᵖᵐ · G, WOODLANDS RD. ILFORD.

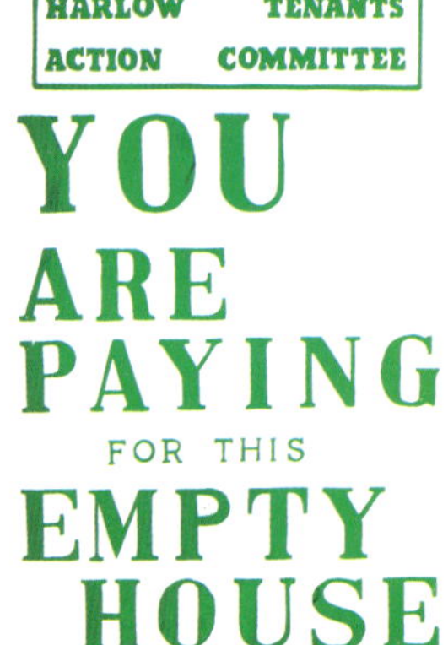

HARLOW TENANTS ACTION COMMITTEE

YOU
ARE
PAYING
FOR THIS
EMPTY
HOUSE

EMPTY
HOUSES

HOMELESS
FAMILIES

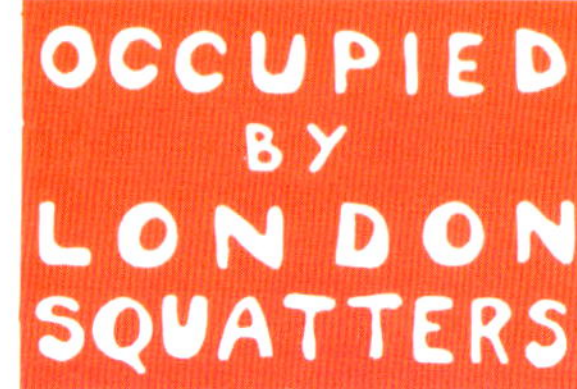

THIS BUILDING IS NOW

OCCUPIED
BY
LONDON
SQUATTERS

IF YOU ARE
HOMELESS
IT'S YOURS

OCCUPY

FREEDOM
ANARCHIST WEEKLY   6d

FIGHTS
FOR THE
HOMELESS

HARLOW TENANTS ACTION COMMITTEE

WHO'S
POCKET
IS YOUR
RENT
LINING

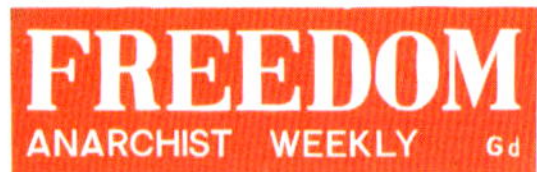

HARLOW TENANTS ACTION COMMITTEE

WHO'S
POCKET
IS YOUR
RENT
LINING

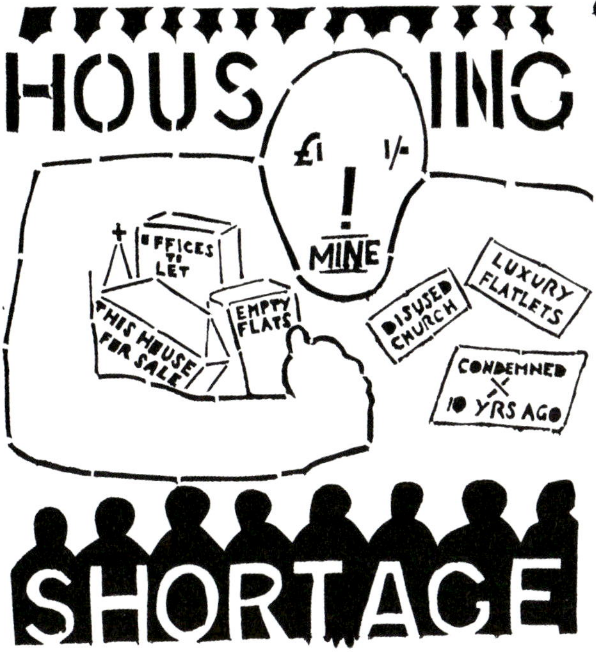

HOUSING
£1 1/-
! MINE
OFFICES TO LET
THIS HOUSE FOR SALE
EMPTY FLATS
DISUSED CHURCH
LUXURY FLATLETS
CONDEMNED 10 YRS AGO
SHORTAGE

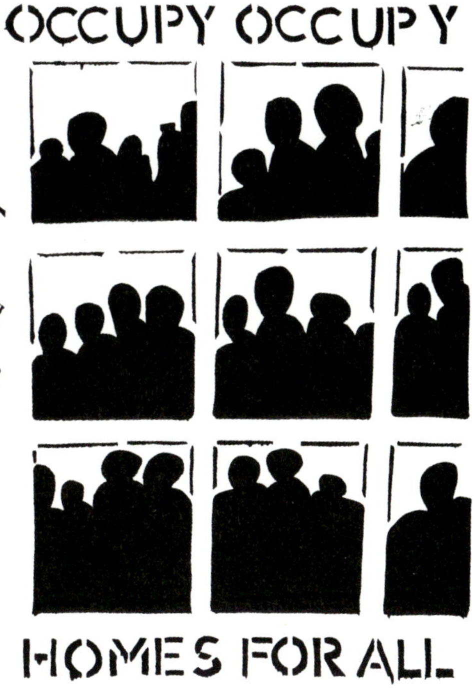

OCCUPY OCCUPY
HOMES FOR ALL

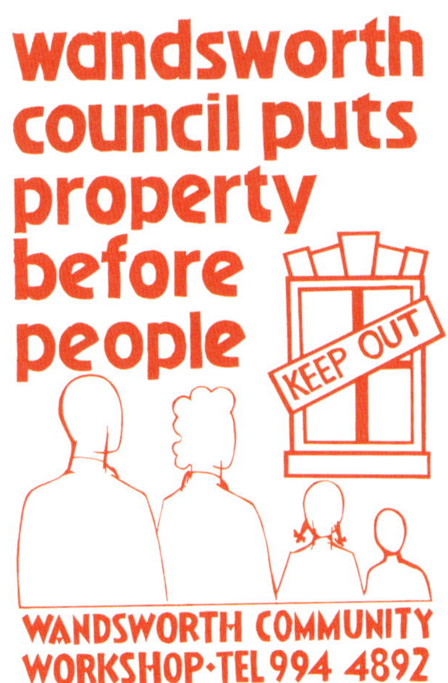

wandsworth council puts property before people
KEEP OUT
WANDSWORTH COMMUNITY WORKSHOP · TEL 994 4892

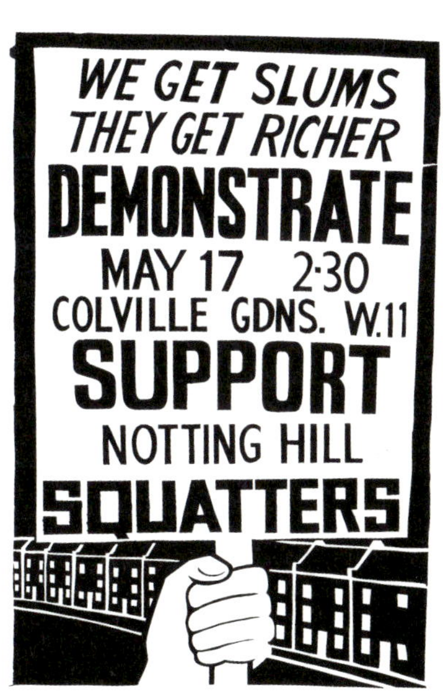

WE GET SLUMS
THEY GET RICHER
DEMONSTRATE
MAY 17   2·30
COLVILLE GDNS. W.11
SUPPORT
NOTTING HILL
SQUATTERS

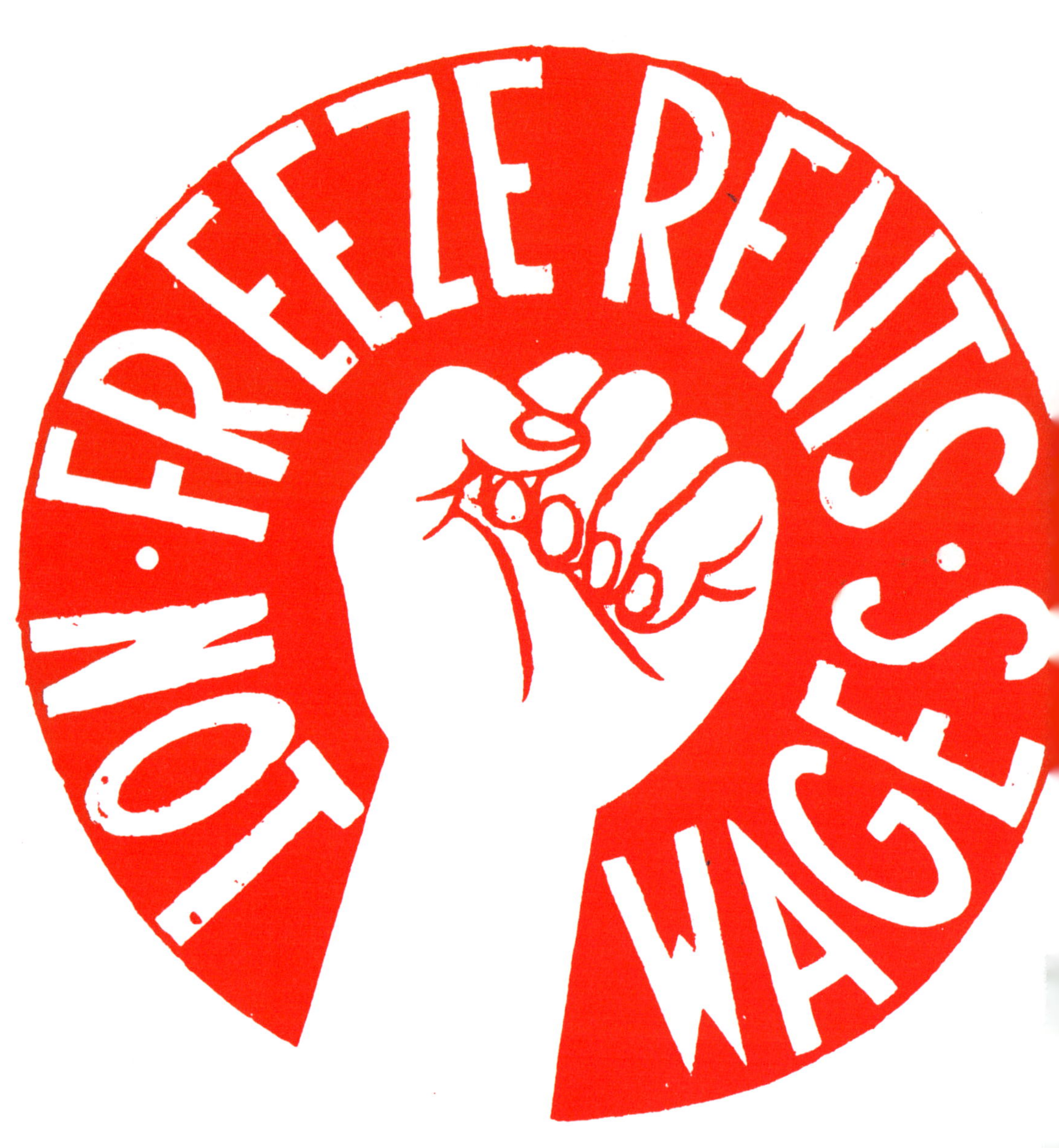

FREEZE RENTS
NOT WAGES

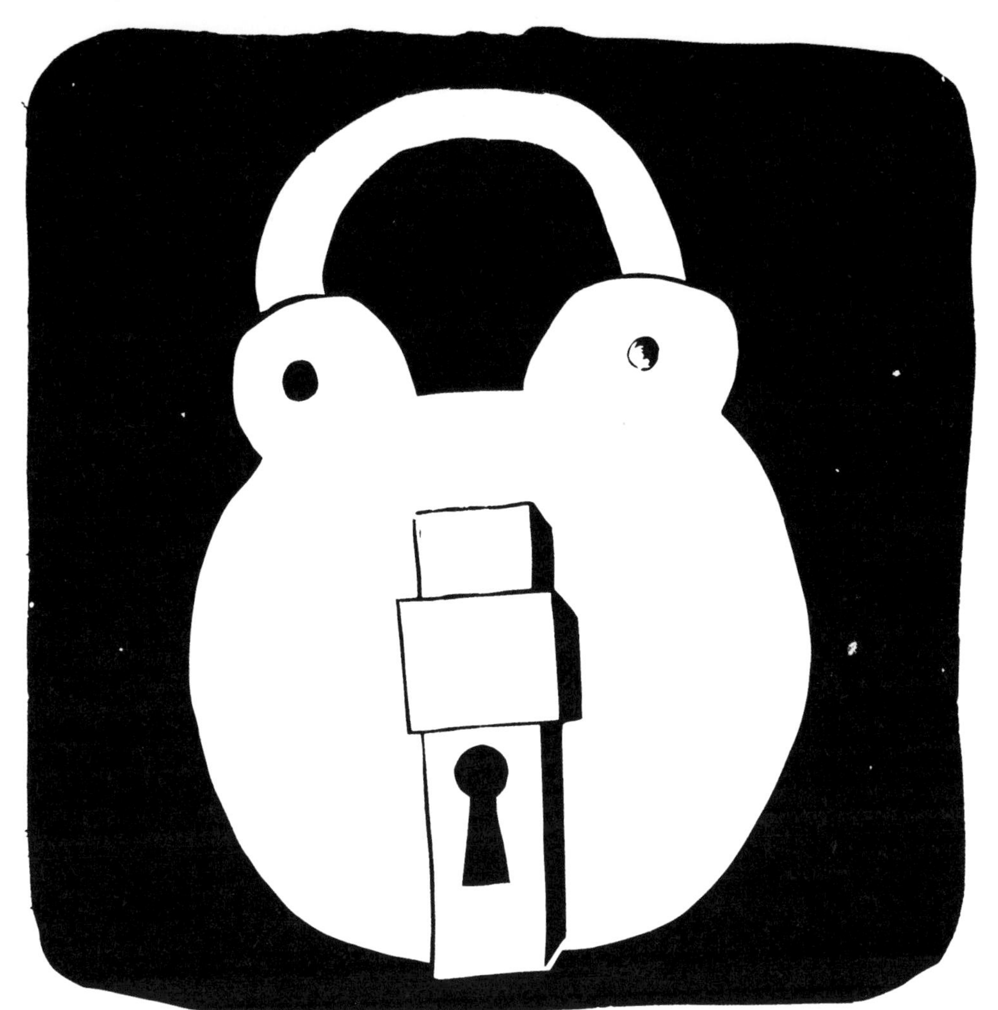

LONDON SQUATTERS
PUBLIC MEETING TO INSTALL
HOMELESS FAMILIES IN EMPTY
PROPERTY. SUN FEB 9TH 2PM
MANOR PARK RD RAILWAY STATION

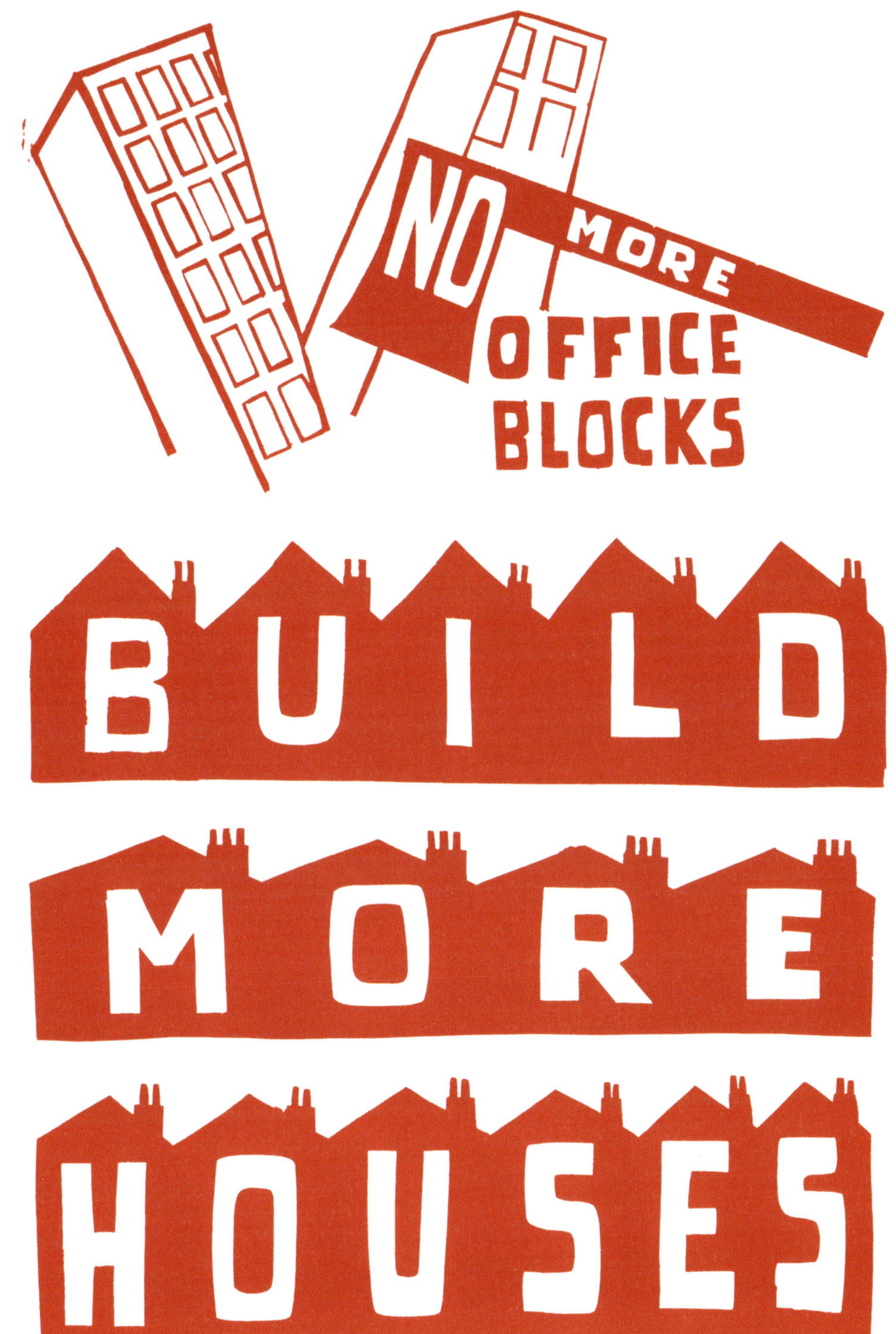

NO MORE
OFFICE BLOCKS
BUILD
MORE
HOUSES

Most of the posters on the following pages were designed by Scriv in support of the 1968–1971 GLC rent strike. Harold Wilson's government, while suffering severe economic depression, had suggested that Local Authorities should charge 'fair rents'.

This idea was taken up with enthusiasm by the Tory Greater London Council, who, in order to reduce financial commitment to the poorer members of society, proposed selling off council housing, ending housing subsidies, and raising rents by 70% over three years. As a first instalment, the rent was set to rise by 25% in October 1968. This led to a mass refusal to pay, mainly in the poor areas of the East End.

In November 1968 local Tenants Associations came together to form the United Tenants Action Committee. These posters show some of the many boroughs in London that were involved in the 'Not a Penny on the Rent' campaign. The *Everybody to County Hall* poster helped to attract 20,000 tenants and trade unionists to the march on County Hall.

Rent Infested (p. 109) was an early poster, printed at Moorhouse Road.

NOT ONE PENNY!
EVERYBODY TO COUNTY HALL
POSTER WORKSHOP 61, CAMDEN RD.
MEET — 7·30, LINCOLN'S INN
LEAVE — 8 PM TUES. NOV. 19
GLC TENANTS ACTION COM.

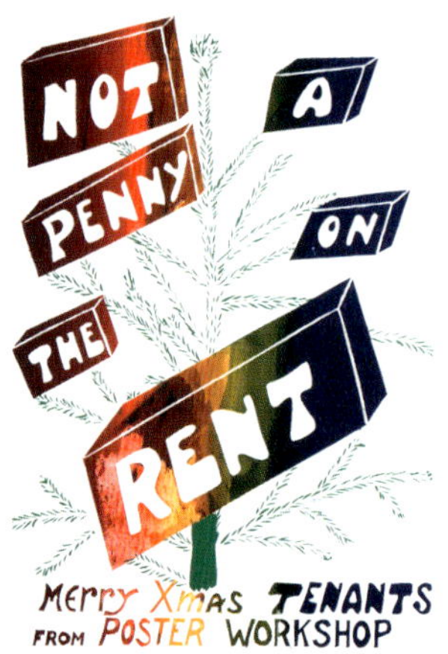

NOT A PENNY ON THE RENT
Merry Xmas TENANTS FROM POSTER WORKSHOP

NO XMAS PRESENT FOR CUTLER
NOT A PENNY ON THE RENT

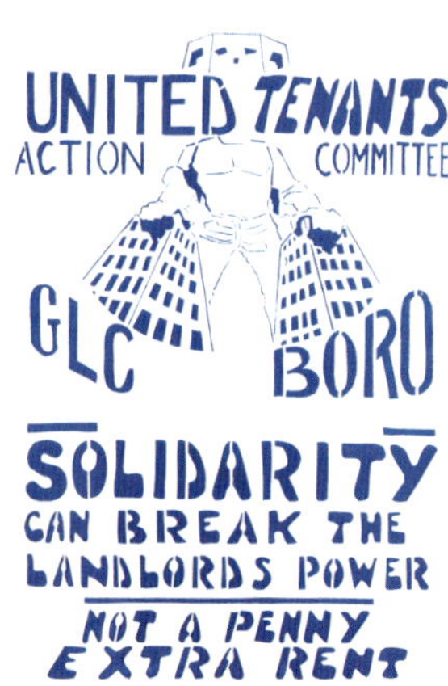

UNITED TENANTS ACTION COMMITTEE
GLC BORO
SOLIDARITY CAN BREAK THE LANDLORDS POWER
NOT A PENNY EXTRA RENT

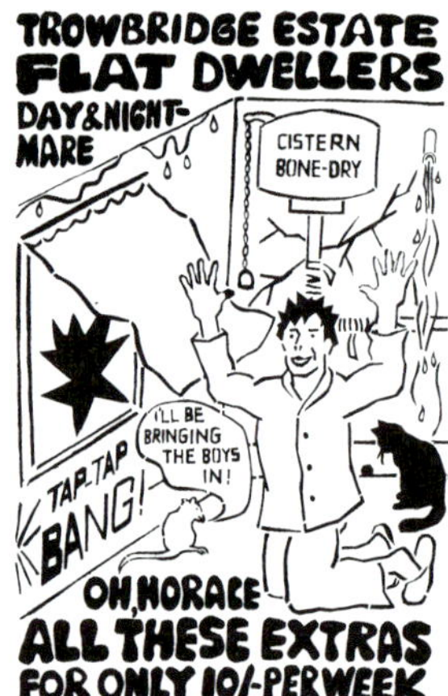

TROWBRIDGE ESTATE FLAT DWELLERS
DAY & NIGHT-MARE
CISTERN BONE-DRY
TAP.TAP BANG!
I'LL BE BRINGING THE BOYS IN!
OH, HORACE ALL THESE EXTRAS FOR ONLY 10/- PER WEEK

HARLOW DEVELOPMENT CORPORATION TENANTS
NOT A PENNY ON THE RENT
NO interest for moneylenders

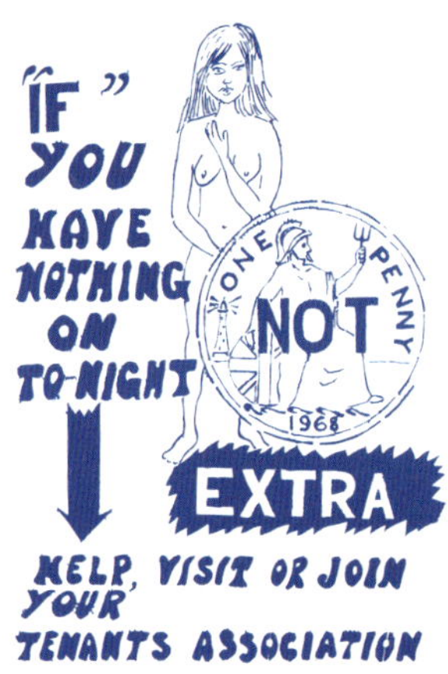

IF YOU HAVE NOTHING ON TO-NIGHT
NOT EXTRA
ONE PENNY 1968
HELP, VISIT OR JOIN YOUR TENANTS ASSOCIATION

UNITED TENANTS MARCH TO SHOREDITCH COUNTY COURT
THEN ON TO COUNTY HALL
MEET AT FRIENDS HALL BARNET GROVE BETHNAL GREEN RD
9·30 AM LEAVE 10·0 AM
29TH APRIL

HOLDING BACK THE RENT RISE?
FIGHT ON!
Remember! 116 GLC Councillors cannot beat half a million united Tenants
RENT FREEZE ICE
UNITED TENANTS ACTION COMMITTEE

TENANTS ASSOCIATION MEETING
"NOT A PENNY" ON THE RENT

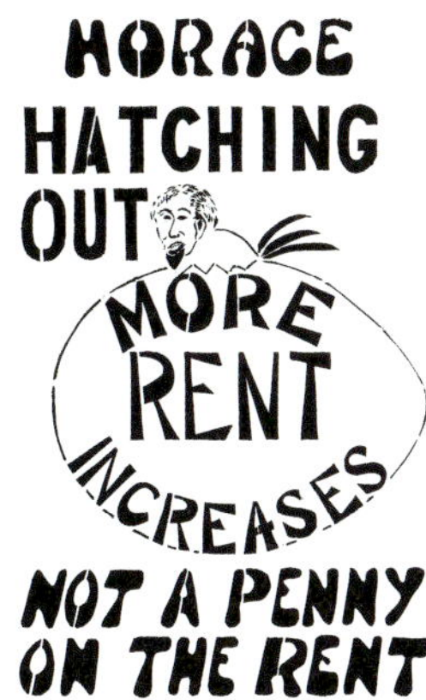

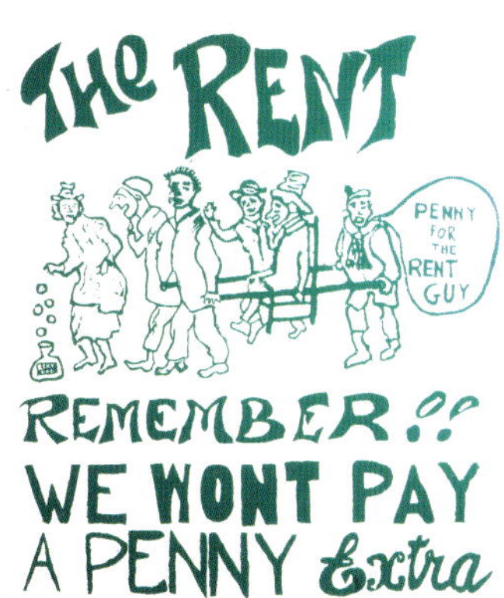

ALL
TENANTS
UNITE

NORTH PECKHAM PROJECT

DISPUTE N° 7

AT COST TO RATEPAYERS
OF
£1800 PER DAY → PLUS
£20000 CONSULTANTS FEE
£900,000 COMPLETION CHARGE
DUE TO
INABILITY OF BOVIS
OR DELIBERATE
REFUSAL TO PRODUCE
A PRACTICAL PRODUCTIVITY
SCHEME FOR
DIRECT LABOUR

CUTLER
MUST
GO

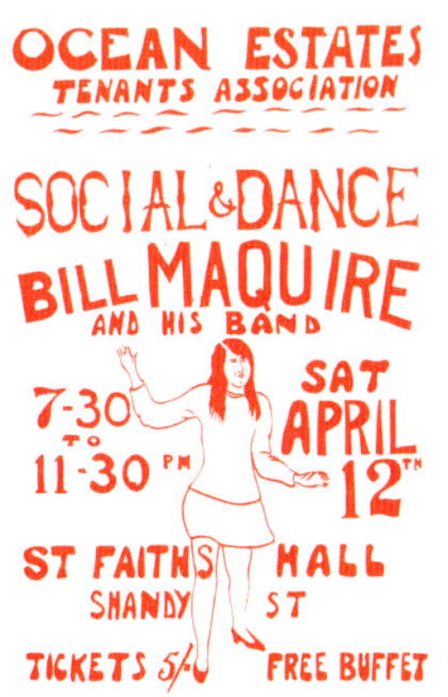

INVASION
SENSATION
!! OF !!
BOREHAM
WOOD
SUN 8TH DEC

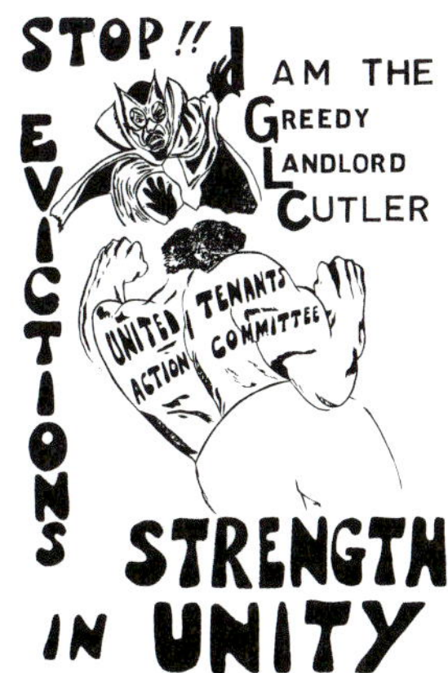

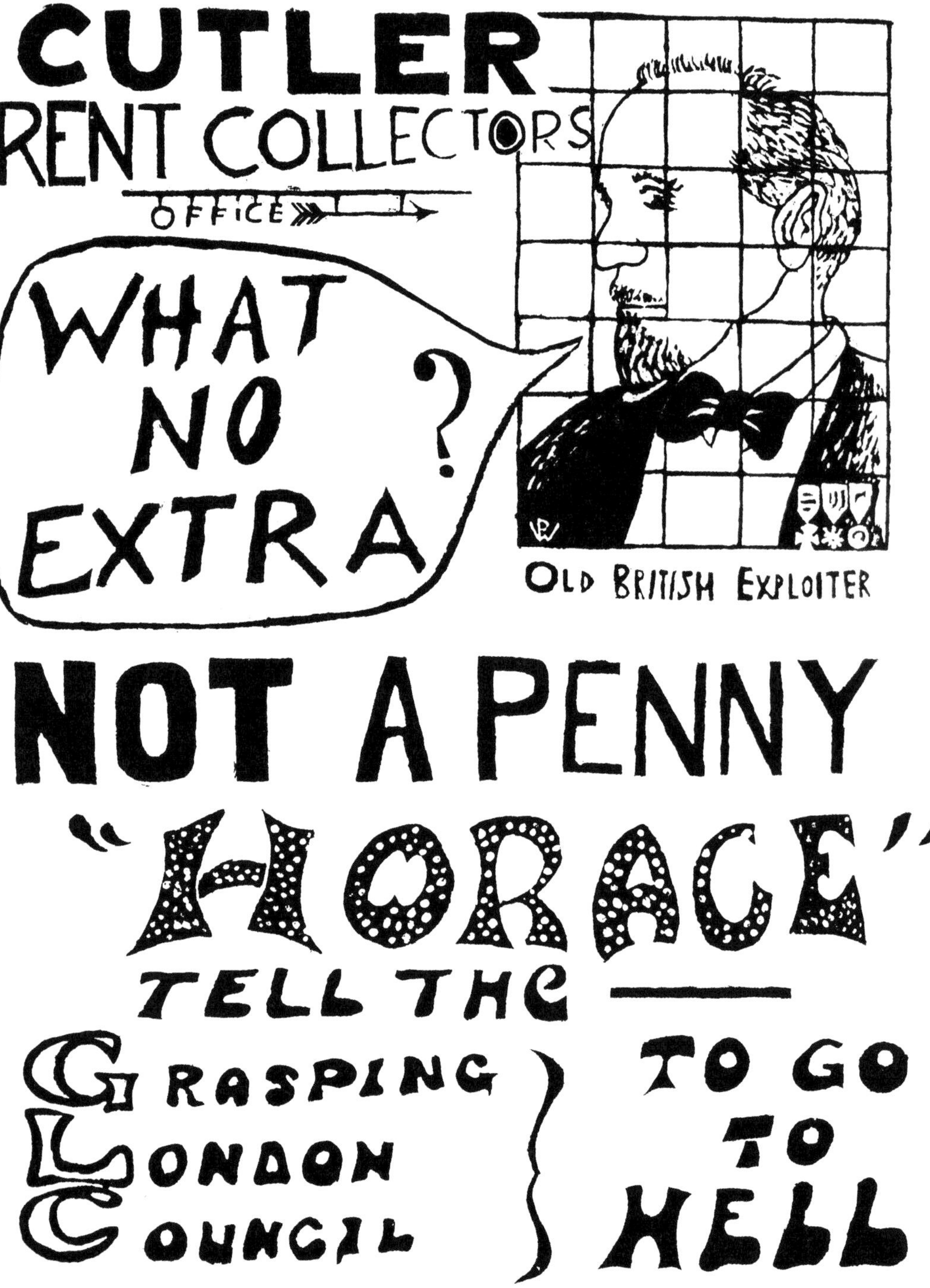

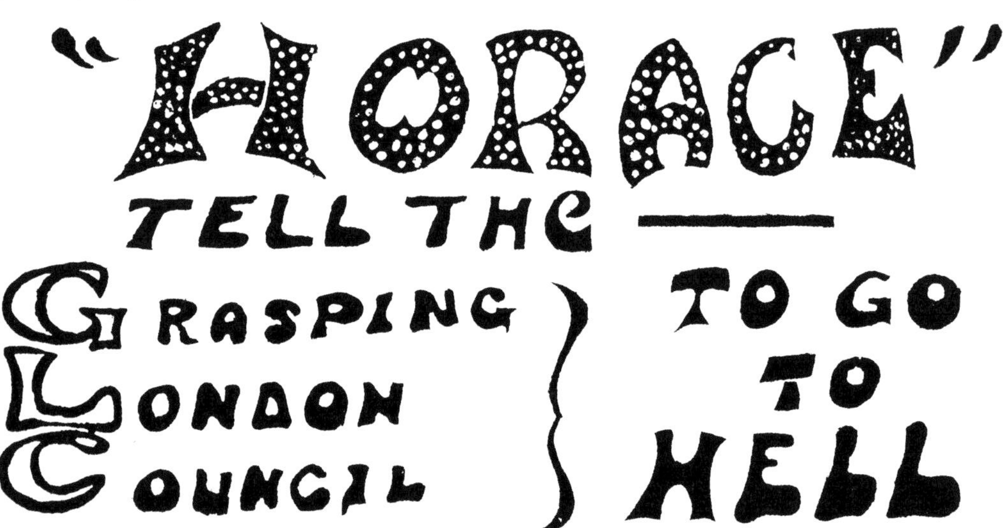

CUTLER
RENT COLLECTORS
OFFICE
WHAT NO EXTRA?
OLD BRITISH EXPLOITER
NOT A PENNY
"HORACE"
TELL THE
Grasping London Council
} TO GO TO HELL

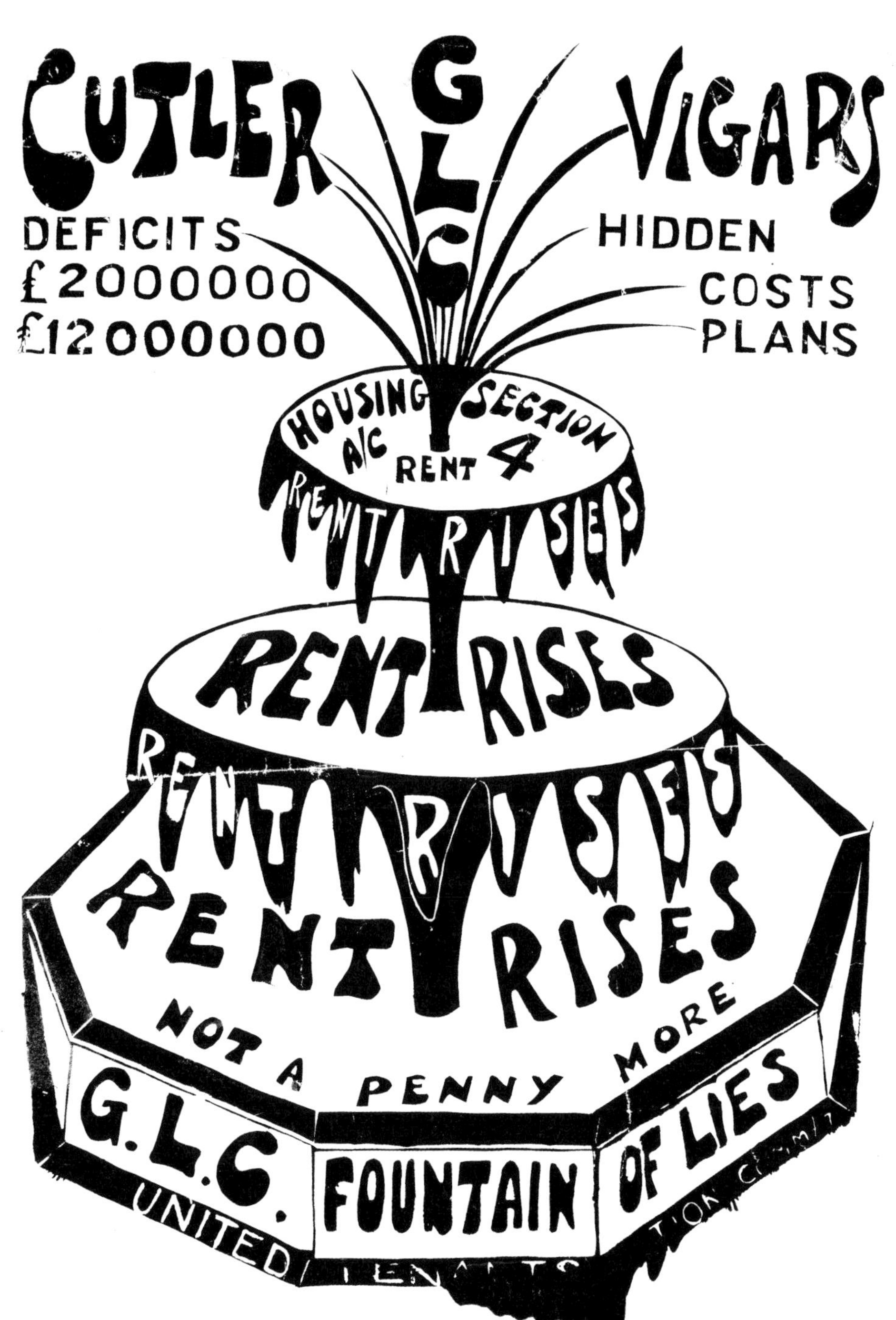

CUTLER
GLC
VIGARS
DEFICITS
£2000000
£12000000
HIDDEN
COSTS
PLANS
HOUSING A/C
RENT
SECTION 4
RENT RISES
RENT RISES
RENT RISES
RENT RISES
NOT A PENNY MORE
G.L.C. FOUNTAIN OF LIES
UNITED TENANTS ASSOCIATION

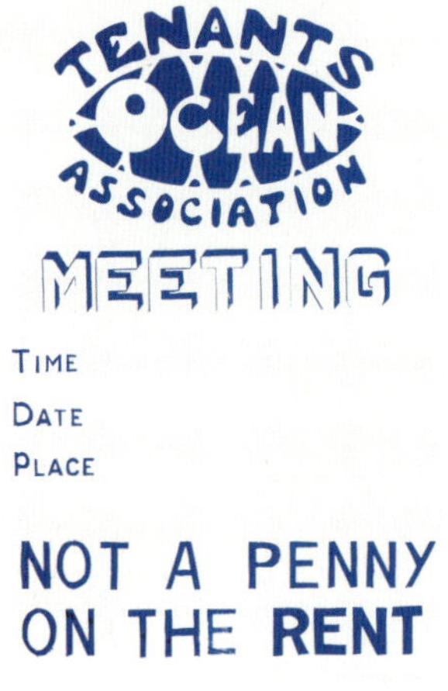
TENANTS
OCEAN
ASSOCIATION
MEETING
TIME
DATE
PLACE
NOT A PENNY
ON THE RENT

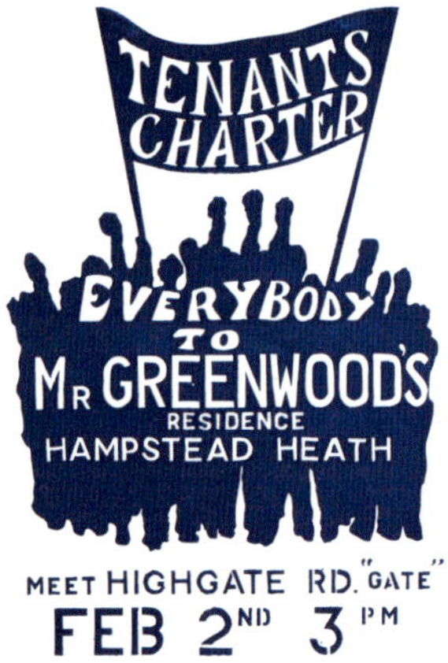
TENANTS CHARTER
EVERYBODY
TO
MR GREENWOOD'S
RESIDENCE
HAMPSTEAD HEATH
MEET HIGHGATE RD. "GATE"
FEB 2ND 3 PM

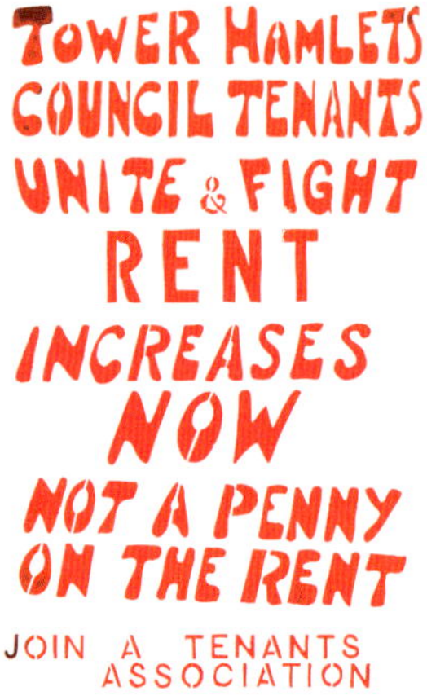
TOWER HAMLETS
COUNCIL TENANTS
UNITE & FIGHT
RENT
INCREASES
NOW
NOT A PENNY
ON THE RENT
JOIN A TENANTS
ASSOCIATION

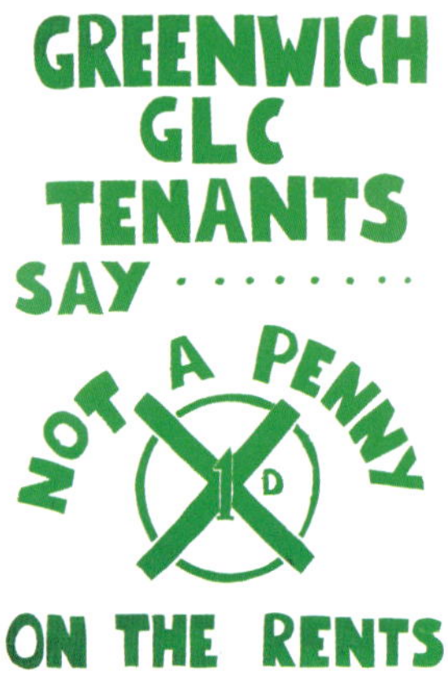
GREENWICH
GLC
TENANTS
SAY
NOT A PENNY
1D
ON THE RENTS

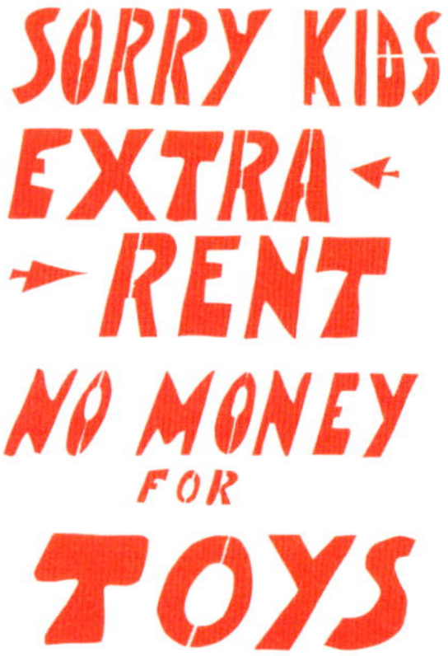
SORRY KIDS
EXTRA
RENT
NO MONEY
FOR
TOYS

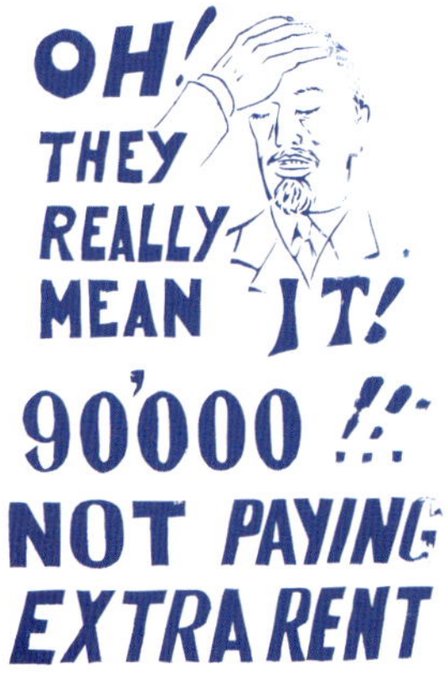
OH!
THEY
REALLY
MEAN IT!
90'000 !!
NOT PAYING
EXTRA RENT

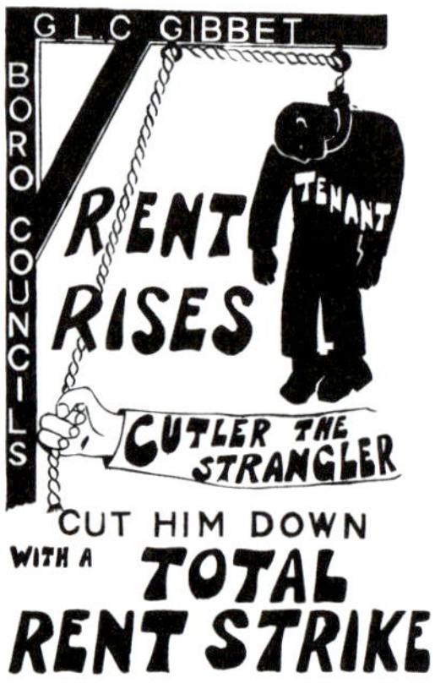
G.L.C GIBBET
BORO COUNCILS
RENT
RISES
TENANT
CUTLER THE
STRANGLER
CUT HIM DOWN
WITH A TOTAL
RENT STRIKE

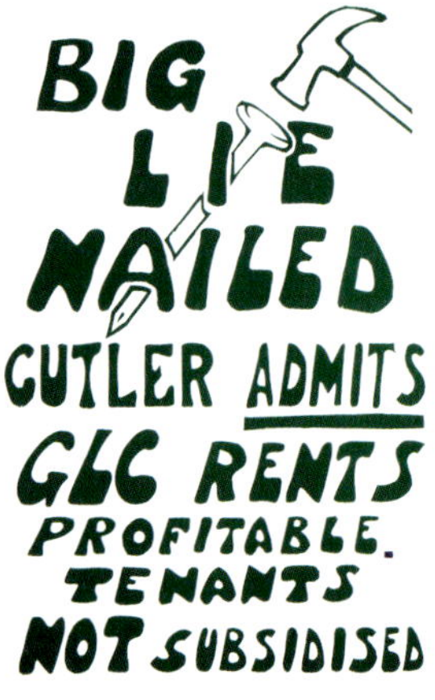
BIG
LIE
NAILED
CUTLER ADMITS
GLC RENTS
PROFITABLE.
TENANTS
NOT SUBSIDISED

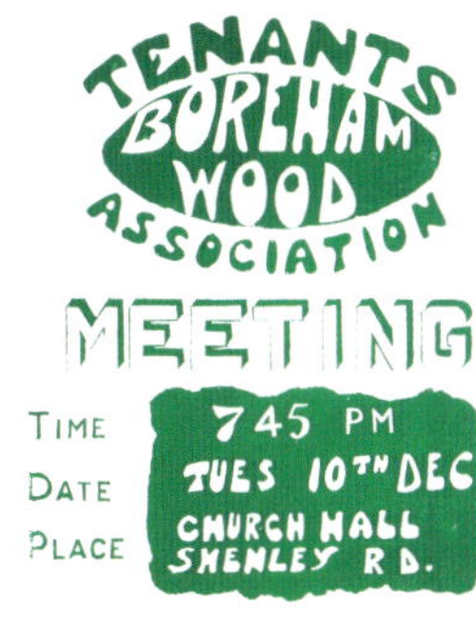
WATLING ESTATE
WHAT 1969
"FORETELL"
MANY FRIENDS WILL VISIT YOU ON JAN 5TH

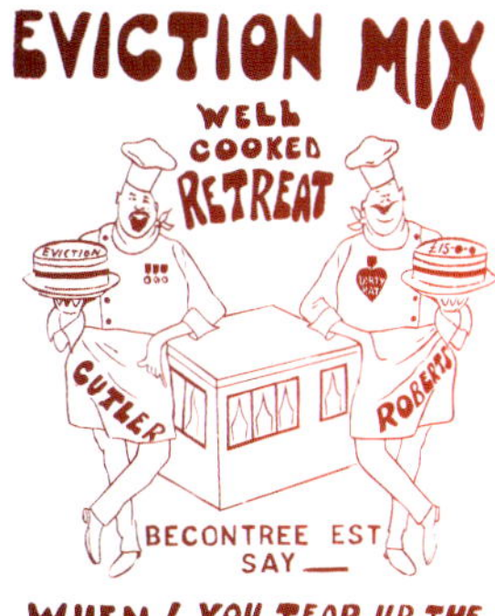
TENANTS BOREHAM WOOD ASSOCIATION
MEETING
TIME 7.45 PM
DATE TUES 10TH DEC
PLACE CHURCH HALL SHENLEY RD.
NOT A PENNY ON THE RENT

EVICTION MIX
WELL COOKED RETREAT
EVICTION
CUTLER
ROBERT
BECONTREE EST SAY —
WHEN! YOU TEAR UP THE POSSESSION ORDER DEFENCES COME DOWN

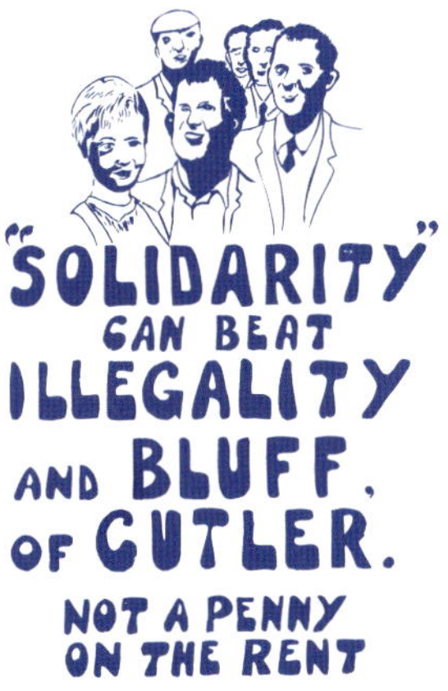
"SOLIDARITY" CAN BEAT ILLEGALITY AND BLUFF. OF CUTLER.
NOT A PENNY ON THE RENT

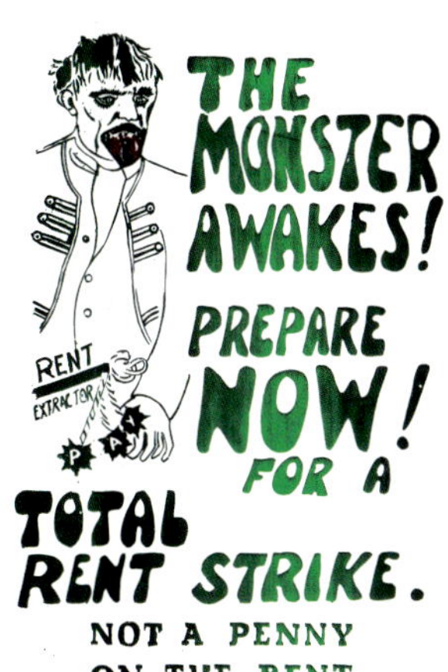
THE MONSTER AWAKES!
PREPARE NOW! FOR A
TOTAL RENT STRIKE.
RENT EXTRACTOR
NOT A PENNY ON THE RENT

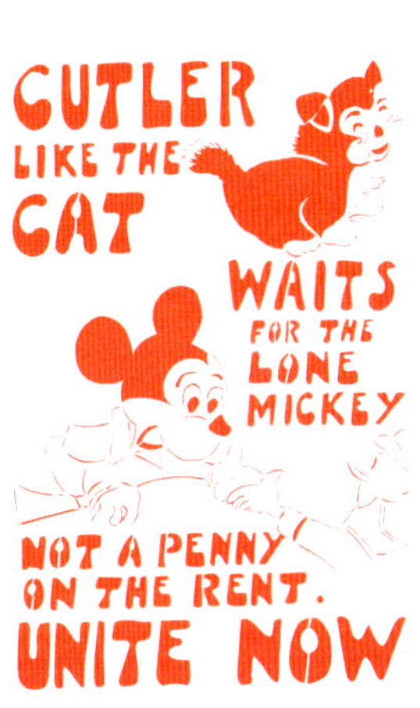
CUTLER LIKE THE CAT
WAITS FOR THE LONE MICKEY
NOT A PENNY ON THE RENT.
UNITE NOW

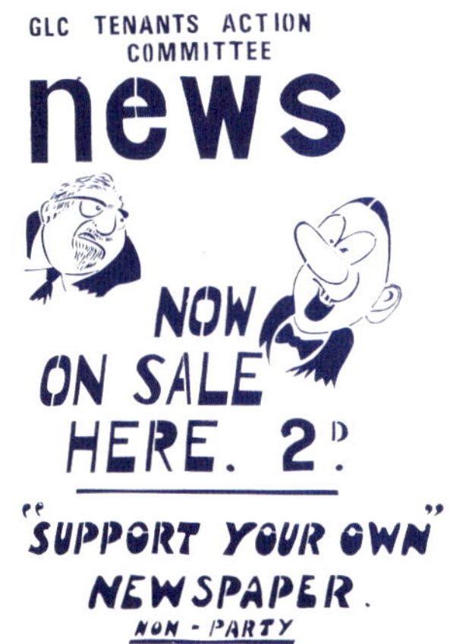
GLC TENANTS ACTION COMMITTEE
news
NOW ON SALE HERE. 2D
"SUPPORT YOUR OWN" NEWSPAPER.
NON-PARTY

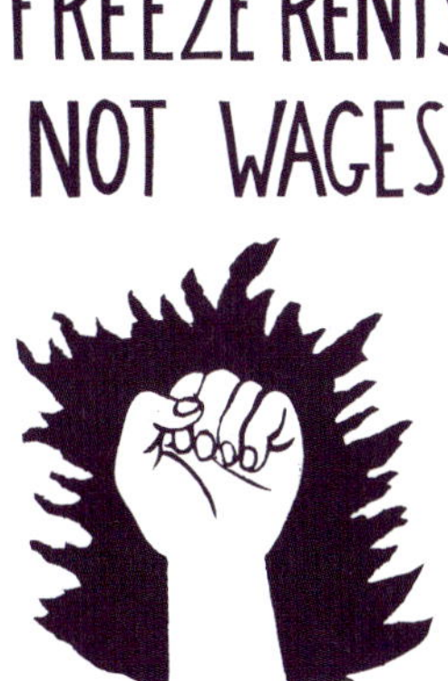
FREEZE RENTS NOT WAGES

EVICT CUTLER

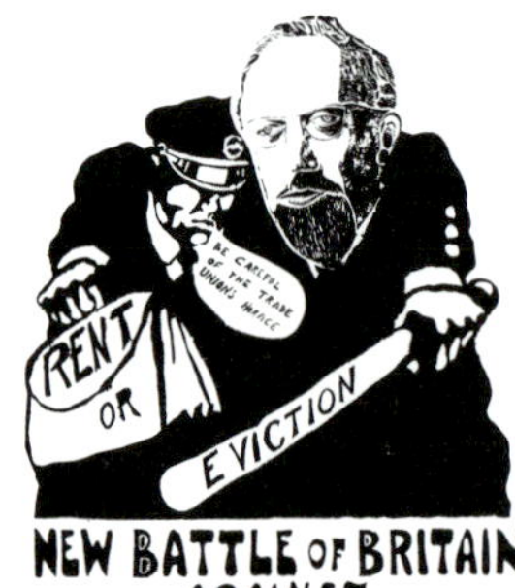

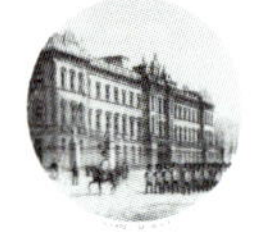

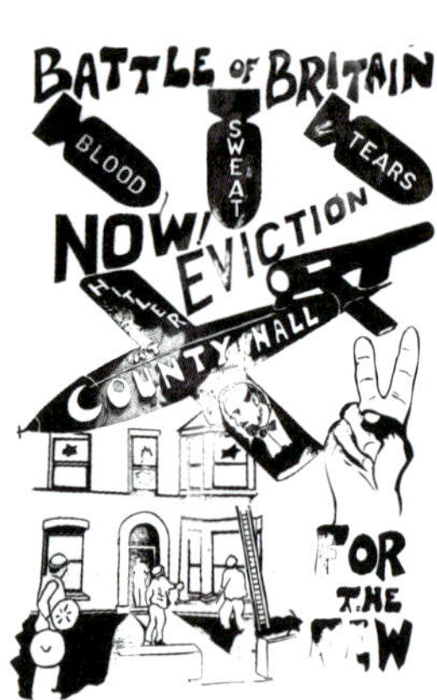

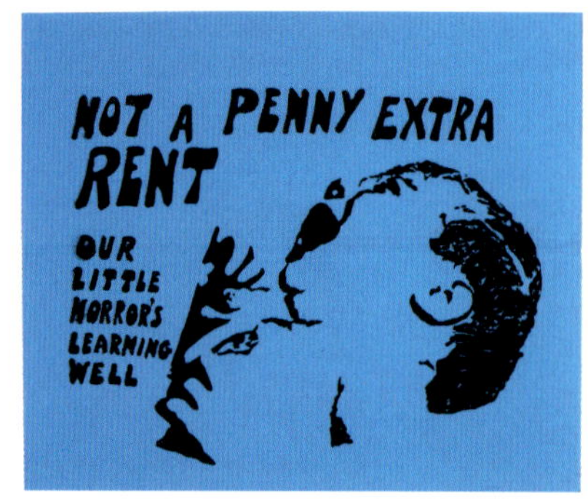

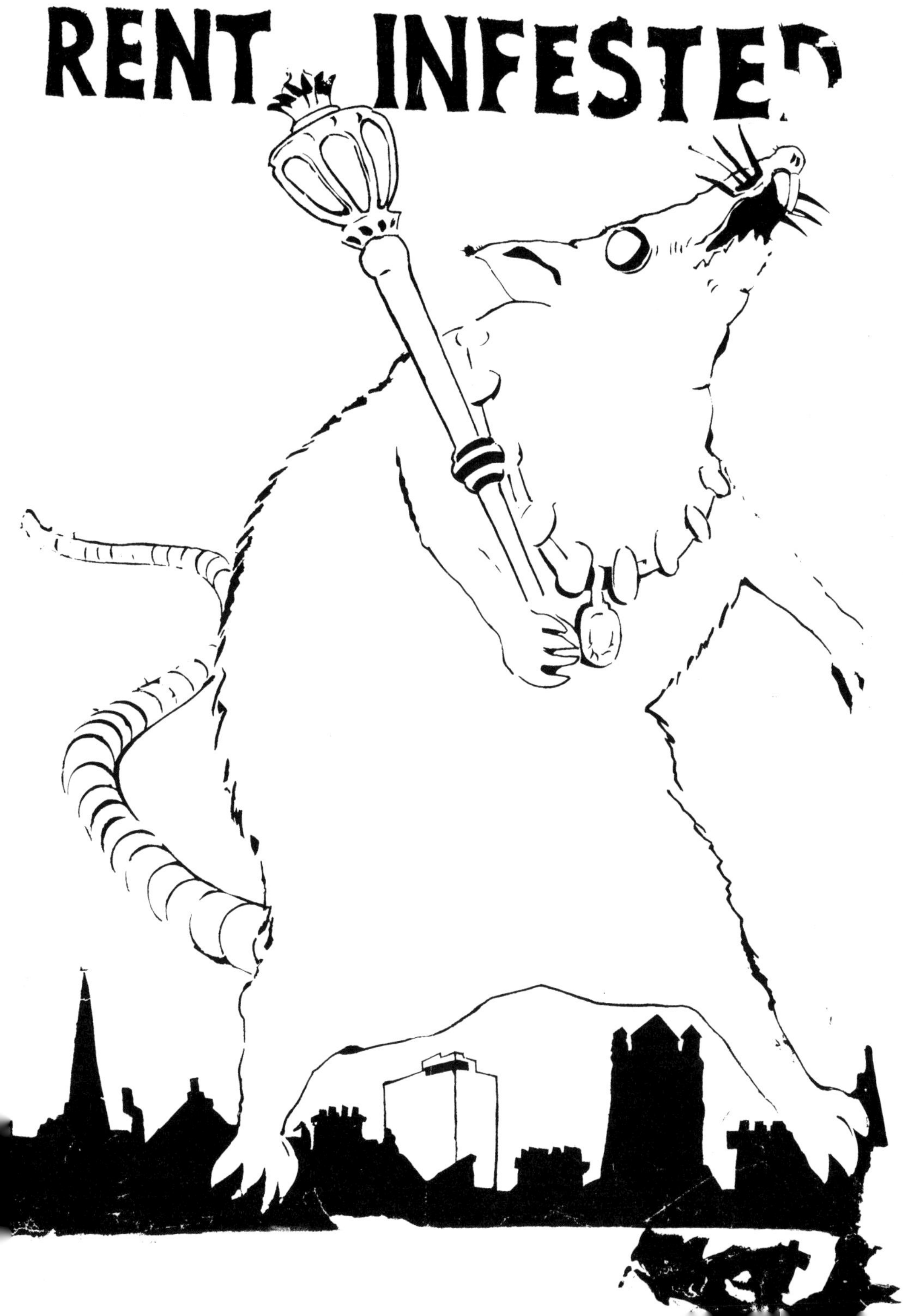

RENT INFESTED

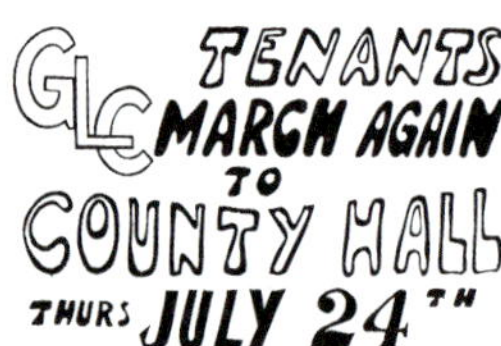

GLC TENANTS MARCH AGAIN TO COUNTY HALL
THURS JULY 24TH
WEST SMITHFIELD MEET 7:30 LEAVE 8 PM
CUTLER – WINING AND DINING AT YOUR EXPENSE
BRASS BAND – MUSIC
FLOATS – FANCY DRESS
DANCING – RENT PLAY
COME AND ENJOY YOURSELF

HACKNEY
NOT A PENNY EXTRA RENT

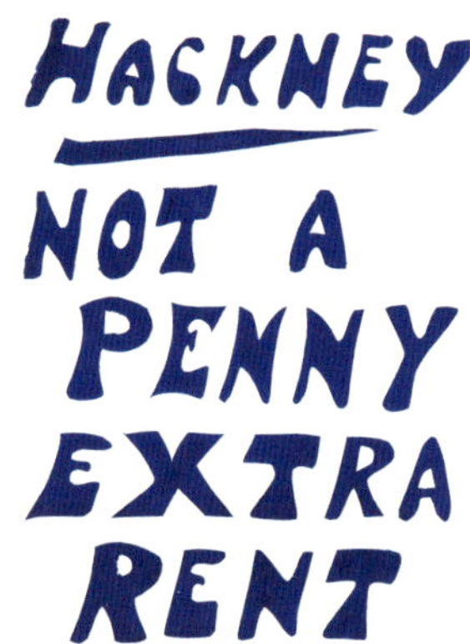

QUEEN'S BLDGS RENT £ £
RACHMANNISM IS ALIVE AND WELL AND LIVING OFF OUR BACKS

OVERCROWDED?
HIGH RENTS?
POOR HOUSING?
DO YOU KNOW YOUR RIGHTS?
WANDSWORTH COMMUNITY WORKSHOP · TEL 994 4892

CUTLERS ERROR
1968 RENT INCREASE → IS ← ILLEGAL
STOP !!! PAYMENTS NOW

TENANTS "JOIN" → YOUR TENANTS ASSOCIATION
NOT A PENNY ON THE RENT

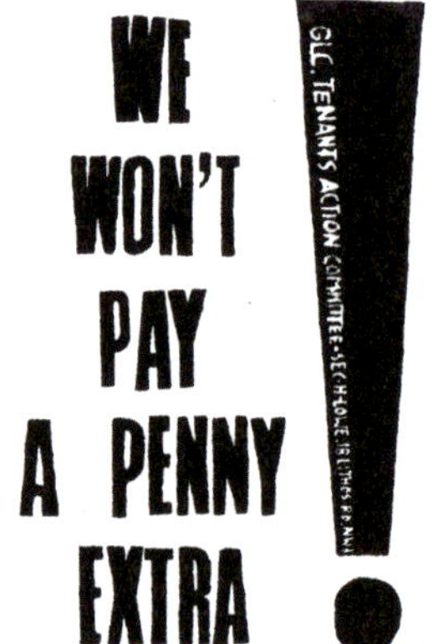

WE WON'T PAY A PENNY EXTRA!
GLC TENANTS ACTION COMMITTEE · SEC H GOLE 18 CUTLERS PENN

SUFFOLK ESTATE
WE ARE NOT PAYING "ARE YOU"
NOT A PENNY ON THE RENT

TO ALL TRADE UNIONS
YOU HAVE A ↑ DUTY ←
TO SUPPORT YOUR MEMBERS FIGHTING RENT RISES & EVICTION
UNITED TENANTS ACTION COMM

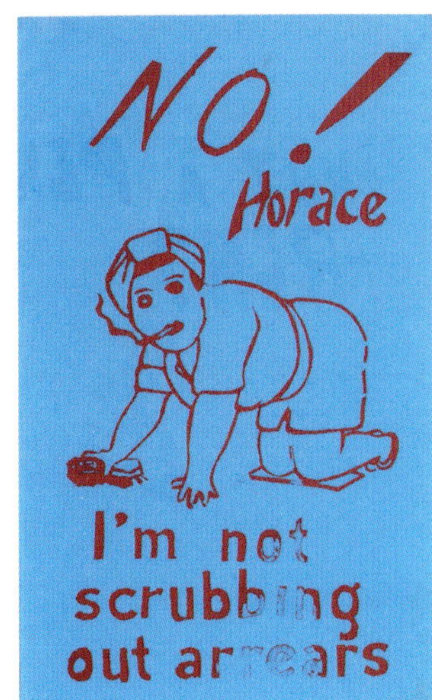

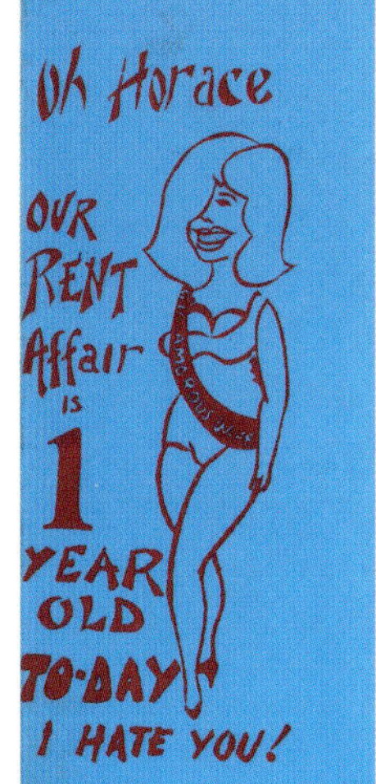

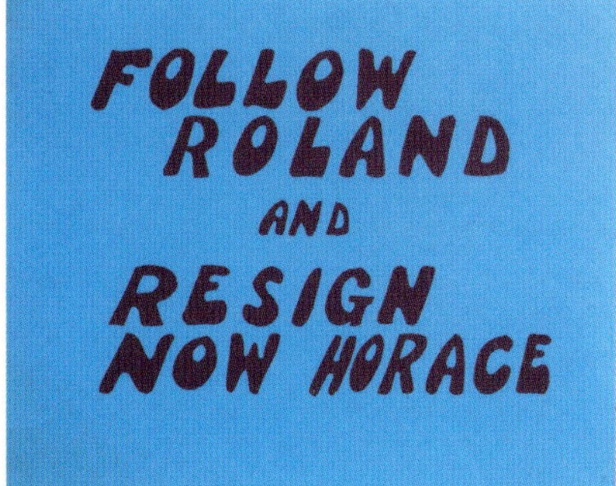

GREENWICH
GLC TENANTS
SAY: CUTLER
OUT! OUT! OUT!

NOT A PENNY
ON THE RENT

LONDONERS!
CAUSE ___ FOR
CONCERN
COUNTY
HALL
MYSTERY
OF THE LAST THREE
RENT RISES
TENANTS DEMAND
PUBLIC ENQUIRY

OCEAN
ESTATE
MEETING

CLUB ROOM

MONDAY

8pm

Meanwhile Ulster began to fester. In 1968, civil rights marches to end 50 years of sectarian discrimination and prejudice under the Protestant dominated Stormont Parliament were violently suppressed by the RUC (Royal Ulster Constabulary) and Protestant paramilitaries. The UVF (Ulster Volunteer Force) exploded bombs and burnt houses, beginning a campaign of ethnic cleansing in Belfast. Catholic areas in Belfast and Derry were sealed with barricades. The Ulster Special Constabulary, commonly called the 'B Specials' (p. 117), were a quasi-military reserve force originally formed just before the partition of Ireland in 1920. They were heavily used to suppress Catholic protests. After much brutality they were disbanded in 1970.

Bernadette Devlin, Irish socialist and republican political activist, was elected to Parliament in 1969 where she represented the Mid-Ulster constituency for People's Democracy until 1974. At that time she was the youngest female MP, at 21, to have been elected to Parliament. In August 1969 British troops were deployed on the streets. At first many Catholics welcomed intervention, but the relationship soon soured when the army was seen to side with the RUC. The moribund IRA (Irish Republican Army) split, partly because of its perceived inability to protect Catholic areas in 1969. The Provos (Provisional IRA) mobilised. The Troubles had begun.

BERNARDETTE DEVLIN

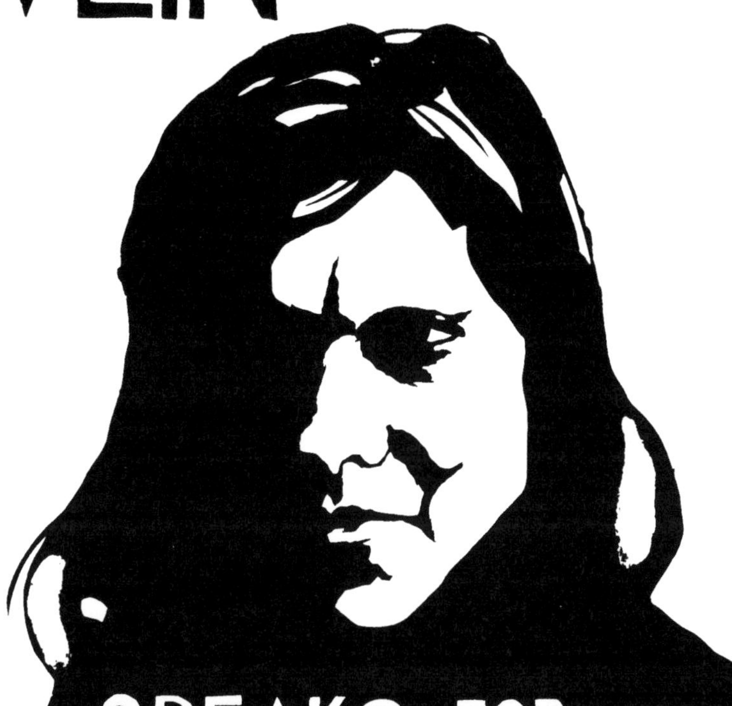

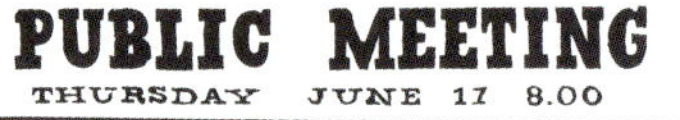
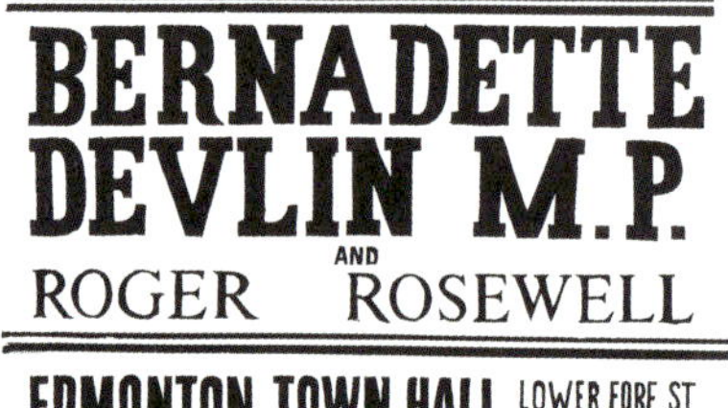
PUBLIC MEETING
THURSDAY JUNE 17 8.00
FIGHT
THE
TORIES
BERNADETTE
DEVLIN M.P.
ROGER AND ROSEWELL
EDMONTON TOWN HALL LOWER FORE ST N.19

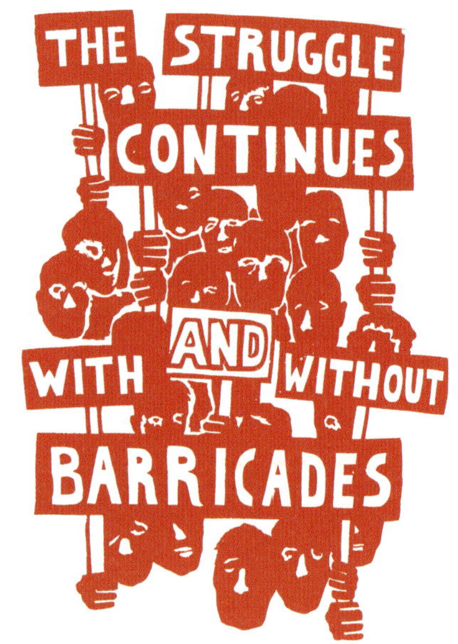
THE STRUGGLE
CONTINUES
WITH AND WITHOUT
BARRICADES

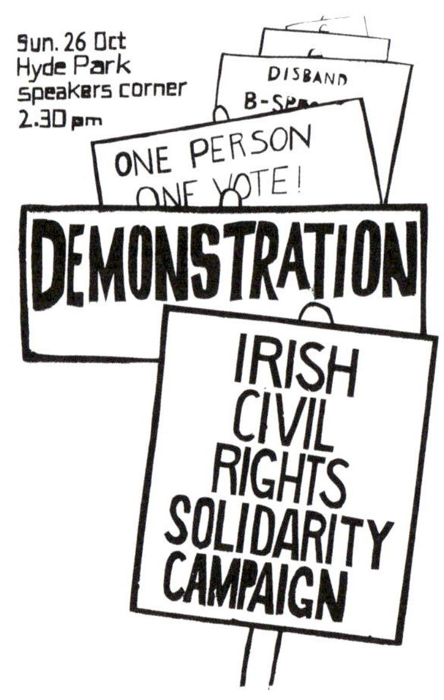
Sun. 26 Oct
Hyde Park
speakers corner
2.30 pm
DISBAND
B-SPE
ONE PERSON
ONE VOTE!
DEMONSTRATION
IRISH
CIVIL
RIGHTS
SOLIDARITY
CAMPAIGN

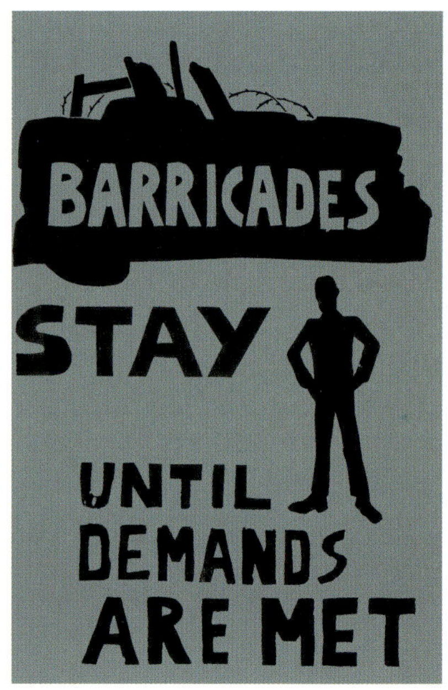
BARRICADES
STAY
UNTIL
DEMANDS
ARE MET

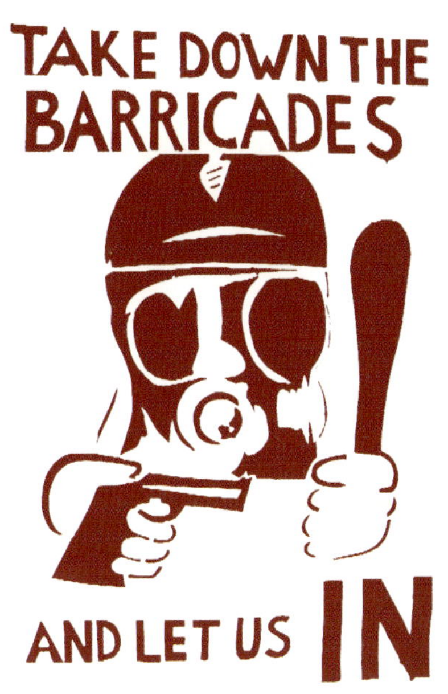

TAKE DOWN THE
BARRICADES
AND LET US IN

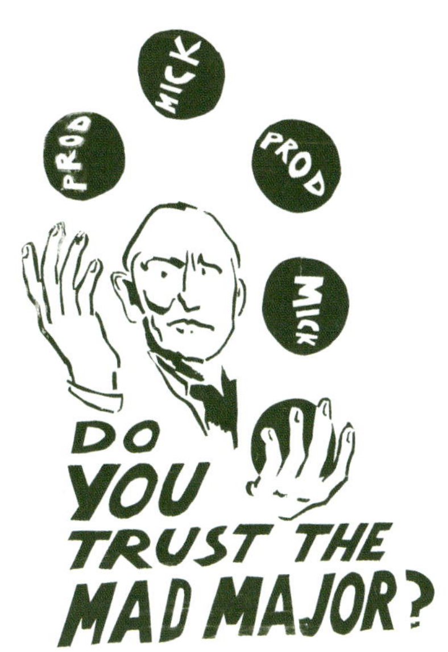

MICK
PROD
PROD
MICK
DO
YOU
TRUST THE
MAD MAJOR?

TROOPS OUT
NOW!
SELF-DETERMINATION FOR
THE WHOLE OF THE
IRISH PEOPLE!

They like
to Be SPECIAL...
UNIONIST PARTY
and have
SPECIAL POWER
to ACT

THE FALLS BURNS

MALONE ROAD FIDDLES

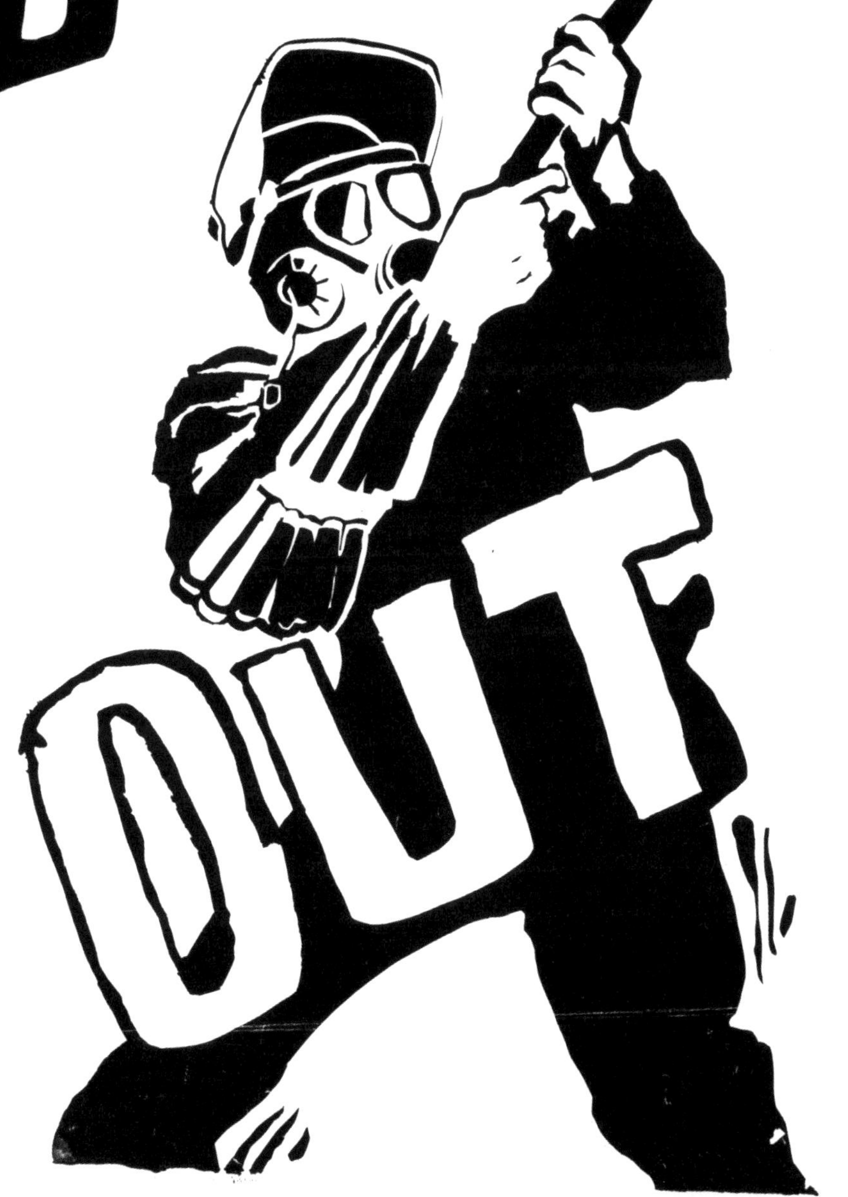

B-SPECIALS
OUT

ARMY
PROTECTION

Legal

Obi Egbuna was a Nigerian Marxist, novelist, playwright, and political agitator. He led the United Coloured People's Association and was a member of the British Black Panther movement. He believed that black people could only gain equality with the overthrow of capitalism. Charged under the Race Relations Act, he was remanded in jail. When he was finally brought to trial, all charges were dropped.

Powis Square (p. 122) was a weed-infested locked garden in the centre of a slum. After a child was run over, a community campaign began to open up the garden. In 1968, dressed as pantomime animals, King Mob headed a crowd that broke down the high fences and finally allowed children to play in the square. It is still a playground today.

FREE
OBI
EGBUNA

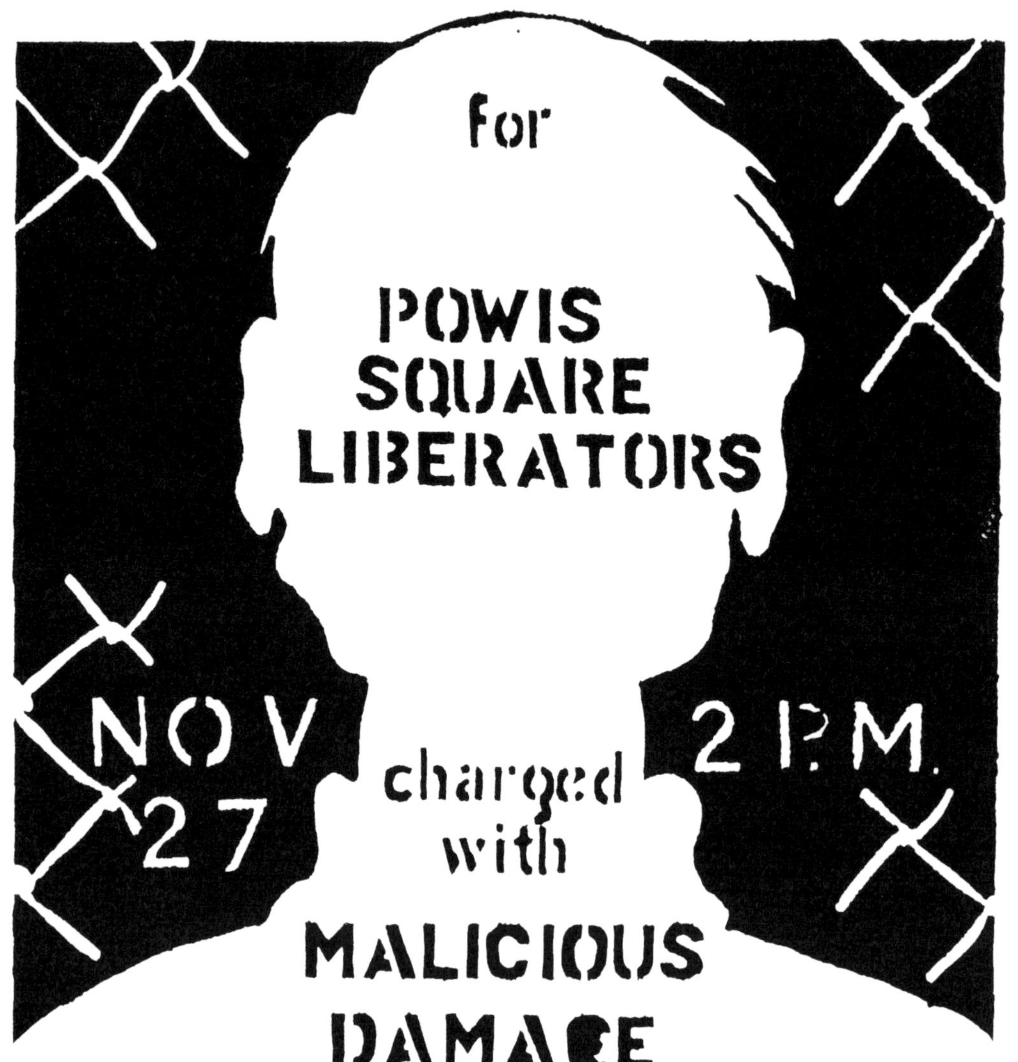

UNITE
for
POWIS
SQUARE
LIBERATORS
charged
with
MALICIOUS
DAMAGE
NOV
27
2 P.M.
MARYLEBONE COURT

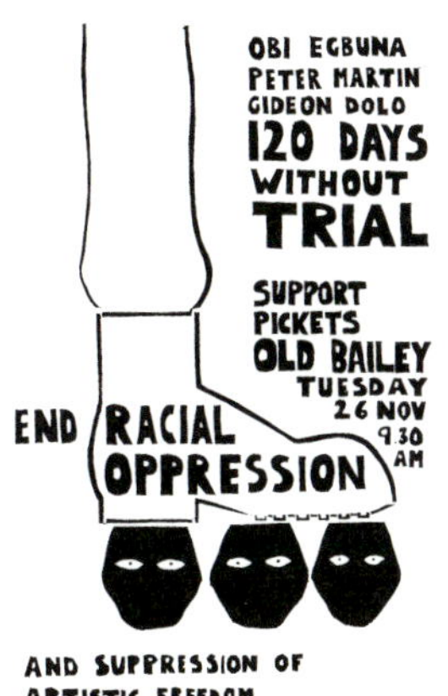

OBI EGBUNA
PETER MARTIN
GIDEON DOLO
120 DAYS
WITHOUT
TRIAL
SUPPORT
PICKETS
OLD BAILEY
TUESDAY
26 NOV
9.30
AM
END RACIAL
OPPRESSION
AND SUPPRESSION OF
ARTISTIC FREEDOM

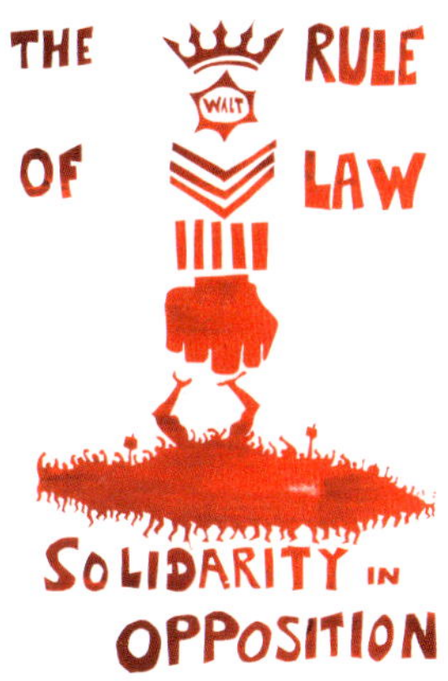

THE
RULE
OF
LAW
WALT
SOLIDARITY IN
OPPOSITION

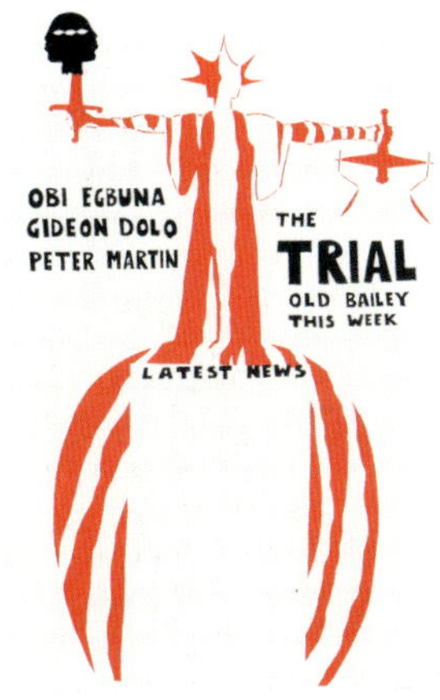

OBI EGBUNA
GIDEON DOLO
PETER MARTIN
THE
TRIAL
OLD BAILEY
THIS WEEK
LATEST NEWS

DEMAND
JUSTICE
AT BOW
COUNTY COURT
10-30
AM
3RD NOV
10-30
AM
96 ROMFORD RD. E14.
MEET — STRATFORD PARISH CH,
STRATFORD HIGH ROAD
ILLEGAL LAW
FOR
LEGAL
POSSESSION

NO TO
STRUGGLE
FOR
RACIAL
INTEGRATION
WITHIN
CAPITALIST
EXPLOITATION

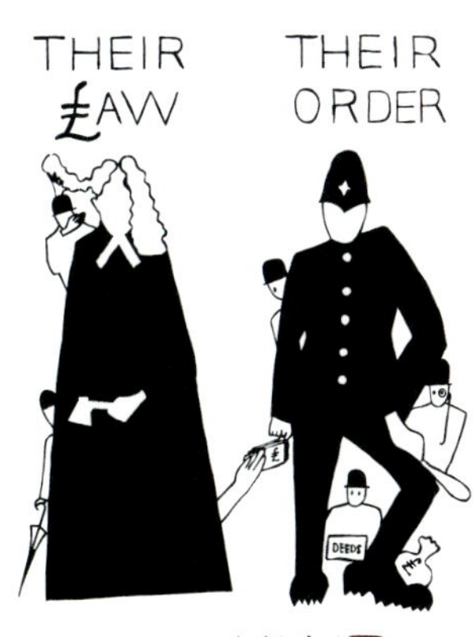

THEIR
£AW
THEIR
ORDER
WE WANT
JUSTICE

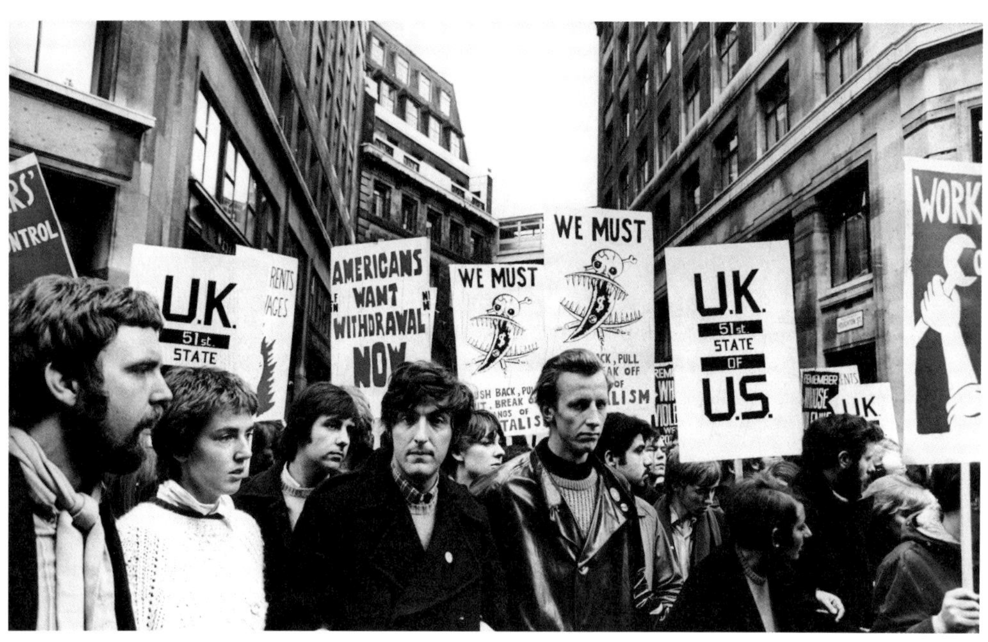
ERS'
NTROL
U.K.
51st
STATE
RENTS
WAGES
AMERICANS
WANT
WITHDRAWAL
NOW
WE MUST
WE MUST
PUSH BACK, PULL
BREAK OFF
OF
TALISM
U.K.
51st.
STATE
OF
U.S.
REMEMBER
WHI
VIOLE
RENTS
WORK

Postscript

The Poster Workshop existed at an exceptional time, thriving on the energy generated by the belief that huge changes were possible, and indeed were already taking place around the world through movements for equality, civil rights, freedom, democracy and revolution. To many it seemed as if capitalism deserved to be smashed, could be smashed and would be smashed. The posters show the extraordinary diversity of those who came to the workshop; they were able to give voice to their outrage. Poster Workshop was a microcosm of much that was happening nationally and internationally at that time – of excitement, change and hope.

Much that has happened in the last 50 years had never been dreamed of in 1968, yet depressingly much remains the same, making these posters still so relevant today. On the one hand, campaigns for women's liberation, racial integration, the acceptance of polymorphous sexuality, the relaxation of censorship, the preservation of the environment and the advances in science and technology have improved the life of millions.

On the other, the debate about economic and social alternatives that were once commonplace are now almost completely excluded from mainstream discourse. Increasing production and productivity at all costs are the mantra. Since the time of Mrs Thatcher, neo-liberalism has steadily eroded the role of the state in the day-to-day business of managing the economy. Democracy is being overwhelmed by unaccountable multinationals and lobbyists. Globalisation has replaced colonialism. The gap between rich and poor has increased enormously. Global warming and other forms of planetary degradation are wrecking our earth which, combined with increasing warfare displaces millions of desperate, hungry people as refugees.

Simultaneously the world of communication has been transformed. Satellites, internet, smartphones and social media spread information at speeds unimaginable at the time of the Poster Workshop. This increased communication could lead to a better world, where our humanity and ability to work together to solve our manifold problems is not based entirely on the need for profit. In our youth we danced for liberty and personal freedom, not the liberty to exploit and oppress, but to turn our dreams of equality into reality. Let's continue dancing!

Poster Workshop

Marching at Aldwych, London during a mass Anti Vietnam war rally, 27 October 1968.

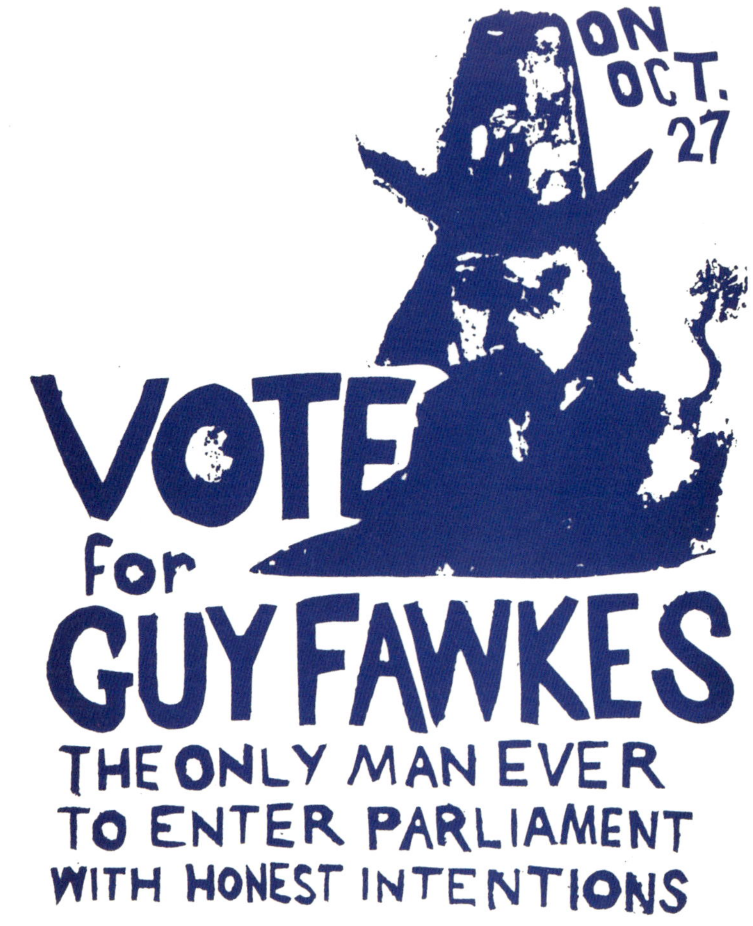

november 1970

sun	1	8	15	22	29
mon	2	9	16	23	30
tue	3	10	17	24	
wed	4	11	18	25	
thur	5	12	19	26	
fri	6	13	20	27	
sat	7	14	21	28	

Acknowledgements

Unbeknownst to the other poster makers, during the life of the Poster Workshop, Peter Dukes collected a sample of every poster printed. Because no other complete or substantial collection of posters has survived, Peter's archive has formed the basis for this book, and the other presentations of the Poster Workshop: Sarah Wilson, in collaboration with Jo Robinson, created the group's website posterworkshop.co.uk. Sam Lord, with the help of Jo, Sarah and Peter, created a limited run book about the collective, upon which this book has been based.

Thank you also to Martin Attwood, Sue Hudson, Detta Kelly, and Billie Old who all designed posters for the Poster Workshop, as well as Valerie Kemp and Bernard who worked there as volunteers. In addition, we would like to thank Simon Farrell who photographed the posters; Geoff Brown for his help sourcing and photographing several of the Northern Ireland posters; and Linen Hall Library in Belfast who supplied a photograph of Smash Stormont, one of many Poster Workshop posters held in their collection.

November, from the Poster Workshop calendar for 1970.